CW00551897

TOWARDS UNDERSTANDING
PUKHTOON JIRGA

An indigenous way of peacebuilding and more.....

by

Hassan M. Yousufzai
&
Ali Gohar

SANG-E-MEEL PUBLICATIONS
25, SHAHRAH-E-PAKISTAN (LOWER MALL) LAHORE.

954.912   Hassan M. Yousufzai & Ali Gohar
                 Towards Understanding Pukhtoon Jirga /
            Hassan M. Yousufzai & Ali Gohar.-Lahore:
            Sang-e-Meel Publications, 2012.
                 112pp. with pictures & map.
                 1. History - Pukhtoon - Politics.
            I. Title.

2012
Published by:
Niaz Ahmad
Sang-e-Meel Publications,
Lahore.

Just Peace Initiatives
772-Hassan Street, Behind VIP Guest House
Old Bara Road University Town Peshawar
Pakistan

ISBN-10: 969-35-2479-9
ISBN-13: 978-969-35-2479-6

Sang-e-Meel Publications

25 Shahrah-e-Pakistan (Lower Mall), Lahore-54000 PAKISTAN
Phones: 37220100-37228143 Fax: 37245101
http://www.sangemeel.com e-mail: smp@sang-e-meel.com
PRINTED AT: HAJI HANIF & SONS PRINTERS, LAHORE.

A Pukhtoon Jirga in Process in South Waziristan Agency of NWFP
January, 2005. Courtesy: "The Nation"

Spin Ziri or White bearded elderly Pukhtoons at a
Community Conference in Afghan Refugee Camp near Peshawar.

Map Showing Pukhtoon Majority Areas
of Pakistan and Afghanistan

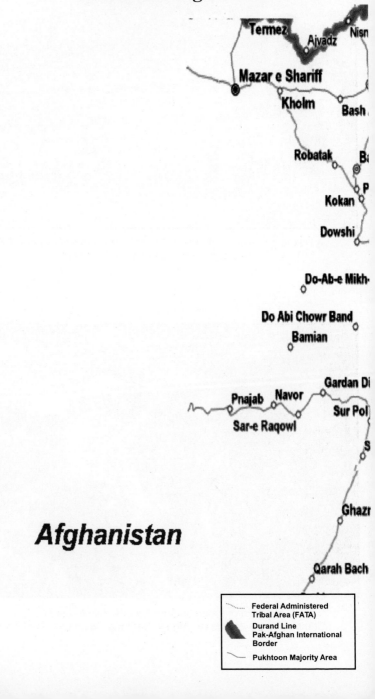

Contents

Many societies have traditional processes with deep historical and cultural roots for maintaining just and peaceful communities. These traditions have enabled societies to function for centuries. Jirga is one of these important traditions. All too often, the modern legal system has ignored or repressed these traditional approaches in the name of modernity and uniformity.

Modern legal systems do have important roles to play in safeguarding human rights and guarding against abuses. Moreover all societies do have both functional and dysfunctional elements. None of our traditions are perfect, and all are forced to adapt as the world changes.

I envision restorative justice as a way to validate and affirm the best of traditional processes such as jirga, within the context of law and human rights. Restorative justice is an affirmation of core values that are important if we are to live together. Rather than emphasizing rules and law, it emphasizes values and dialogue. Rather than focusing on punishment, it focuses on repair of harm. The ultimate goal is to restore or create harmony within our communities.

At its best, restorative justice involves a dialogue about our core values, about the strengths and values of our traditions, about how traditions such as jirga can operate within the changing realities of the modern world.

For this reason, I am very pleased that this important book about jirga, by my friend and colleague Ali Gohar, is being issued in a second edition.

Foreword

A degree of shock never experienced before, the events of Sept. 11, 2001 introduced the world community to terrorism of another kind. Political leadership in the United States of America (US), assisted by their intelligence agencies, was quick to respond to the situation in three ways. Firstly, the leadership felt the need to calm the panicked and anxious citizens and take immediate precautionary measures. Secondly, it devised some short-term initiatives to bring the confidence of the people back as a nation. And thirdly, they took longer-term initiatives to prevent the world from experiencing such traumas in future.

In the immediate aftermath of this incident, the people of the US looked confused and helpless. Prior to these events, Americans could afford to have little concern for the world outside of the US. The reality of terrorism of this magnitude on their own soil forced Americans to stretch beyond their previous mental boundaries. Explanations of this event began to appear. The suicide phenomenon to the people of the developed world seemed to be attributed mostly to a psychological disorder. Then theories of religious fanaticism emerged and, subsequently, the U.S and other members of the world community settled for what many people, communities and nations consider the brutal and blind response of military force. In the war on terrorism, the only visible target was Osama Bin Laden, a native Arab and a one time strong ally of the US secret services, who later turned against the US government policies. We were told that this person was residing in Afghanistan. Afghanistan became the first battleground for this new war on terrorism.

We, the principal researchers of this work, belong to Peshawar in Pakistan, a place just a few miles away from the Pak-Afghan border. We speak the Afghani language as our mother tongue. A few days before September 11, 2001, we landed in the US as Fulbright Fellows to study Conflict Transformation at Eastern Mennonite University (EMU) in Virginia. As Pakistanis and Muslims—probably the only two Muslims at a Christian university—we suddenly found ourselves barraged with questions from common Americans. Media people rushed to find Muslims in their area. University colleagues came with bundles of questions and community groups invited us for talks.

As we tried to respond to their difficult and often highly technical questions, we noticed that the questions generally centered on three themes:

- Who were the suicide bombers?
- Why they did this to us?
- What should we do now?

To the first question, no one had an immediate answer, but it was clear from the statements of national leadership that the attackers were Muslims and they were friends of Osama. To the second question, the national leadership devised a new theory of terrorism, a term previously used to describe acts of indiscriminate violence within a national or domestic framework. To the third question, no one had a clue.

With the natural bias for peace and tolerance, the EMU community prayed for the victims, gave lots of support to us, and continued to ponder the above questions. To the Mennonites, violence in the name of peace or security is unjustifiable—a stance with which many people in government do not agree. It was under these circumstances that we, as Muslims and Pakistanis of Afghan origin, were expected to give satisfactory answers to our American fellows.

Our understanding of conflict, as students of peacebuilding, is that conflict is an opportunity to address the long-standing issues between parties. In conflicts, violence is used either as an act of vengeance or as a source of communication from one party to the other. Violence to us is a phenomenon, which will invariably attract further violence at least in the long run.

To respond to the above three questions, we started with the basics. The first question, while a matter of scientific investigation, called us to remain cautious, as we may never knew the clear identity of the perpetrators. In addition, we bore in mind that the perpetrators may be perceived as martyrs by others in the world.

The second question to us was not a simple one either, but it was clear that the act was not carried out to just destroy buildings and kill innocent civilians: the act definitely carried a deeper message and symbolism. This looked more like a communication of another kind in which parties did not seek to understand each other. Perhaps the

parties in this conflict did not have any other platform on which to put
their issues before the other for discussion. Or perhaps one party was
too strong and arrogant to pay heed to the concerns of the weaker
party.

To the last question again, our understanding remains that an act of
violence will beget further violence; therefore for a U.S response of
military force against Osama Bin Laden and the Afghani people will
not lead to a cessation of terrorism. The question of what action
should be taken in response to the September 11 hijackings leads us
back to the second question: why did these hijackings occur? What is
it that the U.S needs to understand about Osama's violent form of
communication? Violence is not only a psychological disorder. A party
operating from a place of fear and insecurity may resort to violence
when unable to communicate a message and feel heard through a
verbal medium.

As the US-led attack on Afghanistan to hunt Osama became imminent,
we argued that, in order to achieve strategic objectives, there was a
need for peaceful dialogue with the people of Afghanistan, as opposed
to the use of force. Regular diplomatic norms of the nation state
system were not possible, however, as the US did not formally
recognize the Taliban government. Our suggestion to the US policy
makers was to try to utilize the indigenous Afghan social institution of
Jirga as a forum to sort out all outstanding issues between war trodden
people and one of the most powerful governments of the world. In
the US, there was little enthusiasm for this because of many factors. It
appeared that the US government was in a hurry to launch an offensive
on helpless Afghan people because it was the quickest remedy to the
painful experience of September 11. As EMU professor and conflict
transformation practitioner, Ron Kraybill, would always remind, "If a
hammer is the only tool in your box, everything will look like a nail".

Having lived under a civil war for three decades, the people of
Afghanistan were once again destined to face effects of collateral
damage, a term so easy to pronounce, but so difficult to afford. Yet, at
the end of the day, the US Government invited a national conference
of Afghans, called a Loya Jirga, at Bonn in the spring of 2002.
However, the Bonn Jirga was held without getting a hold of Osama,
the suspected mastermind of September 11 attacks.

Politics and sociology must go hand in hand, as both affect the destinies of common people living in the global village. Where politics bring change in the societies, sociology must enable people to adjust to positive changes. In the absence of a formal political platform, the Afghan culture allowed a quick formation of Loya Jirga, a quasi-political and quasi-social institution, which enabled the war trodden people to get back to a socio-political order of some kind. What would have happened if the Pukhtoon culture didn't have this tradition? Does the nation state system provide for a contingency where a nation can make a peaceful start without any formal institutions? Why is it necessary to identify and respect such cultural understandings not included in the systems of political science? As these questions arose, we felt the need to describe what Jirga is and how it operates. Is it an outdated and obsolete institution or it is capable to face challenges of the present day systems?

We are obliged to the US Institute of Peace for encouraging us to work more on the subject and sponsor our two years of research work in the field. We also thank the Mennonite Central Committee (MCC) for adding partial funding for the project. We went out to talk to over two hundred people who are associated with Jirga in one way or another. The journey took us across all the Federally Administered Tribal Areas (FATA) of NWFP (North West Frontier Province), settled districts of the province, the Pukhtoon districts of Balochistan Province, and a few provinces of Afghanistan, including Kabul and Jalalabad. As this is the very first work to explore the dynamics of Jirga, an effort is made to touch only the very basics of Jirga. This work is an overview of the whole system of Jirga, so as to present a comprehensive and focused work on this long neglected, but well tested, indigenous institution that has influenced the lives of millions of Pukhtoons over hundreds of years of its history.

Many people helped develop this work along the way. The project leader Vernon Jantzi gave us lots of technical input from time to time, while Janice M. Jenner helped us work on designing the project proposal and looking after the budget side. Amy Potter helped us consolidate our work and present it for publication. Our domestic associates include hundreds of people who agreed to spare their precious time, some in pre-organized sessions and others at informal chats, to talk to us on Jirga. Supper talks with elders and peers vastly enriched our understanding of the processes involved in Jirga. We duly acknowledge the value of information on Jirga put up on the Internet by many freelance as well as professionals which has been used to improve our understanding of Jirga. We remain thankful to the proprietors of all those web sites we used during the course of our inquiry. Special contributions of Ikram Hoti, Usman Yaqub, Javed Akhtar, Askar, Nadia Shams, Kashif Karim, Memoona and Noor Akbar Khalil helped with final compilation of work. Kirstin Rothrock's hard and timely help enabled to give final shape to the document. We sincerely thank all our associates, colleagues and peers without whose contributions; this work would not have been possible.

Hassan M Yousufzai & Ali Gohar
January 2005

Introduction

In the face of the modern age of globalization, how should we treat old and indigenous social institutions? What happens when new and more scientific social sector institutions try to override the old and traditional patterns of a society and force them to change? Is there a way in which the new, more dominant, and of course more codified systems benefit from and collaborate with the traditional systems to bring forward the synergies of two different sets of understandings?

For the students of political science and international relations, the nation state system, through the instruments of democratic governance, should ensure continued progress and growth of societies. A sociologist, however finds enormous richness in the traditional and indigenous social mechanisms, which are duly credited for carrying the societies through the difficult periods of their history, giving them energy and helping them go on. This very practical aspect of traditional practices, combined with the love and appreciation indigenous people have for the past, gives indigenous people the confidence needed to continue to utilize their traditional institutions.

The meeting point between the new and the old systems therefore is of critical importance to those who wish to see things right. The negotiation between the two must meet the standards of justice if the change desired is to be positive and sustainable. The western democratic system brings with it many new ideas of equity and social justice. Its task then becomes selling these new ideas to the older generations and remote societies in such a way that they find advantage in leaving behind their rich and inherited cultures. In the process, many of the old practices that are rooted in local wisdom are discarded as people seek out the better life promised in the modern systems. What is often neglected is how the ancient traditions and practices can inform the modern systems.

The Pukhtoon Jirga is one such institution, which according to modern standards of governance, apparently seems to have outlived its utility. Yet an overwhelming majority of people living under this system, sing its praises. The latest example of the Loya Jirga at Bonn in the spring of 2002, used to form an Afghan national government after three decades of civil war, is a good example of use and viability of traditional institutions. In this Afghan scenario, when nothing else worked, the people of Afghanistan put their trust in a Jirga to help them recover from a state of anarchy and decide for their future. Suddenly, the Loya Jirga—its history, procedure, and jurisdiction—became visible to the greater world community.

Historically a people of unique characteristics, Pukhtoon societies have held the concept of Jirga quite sacred to them and have allowed this institution to rule them throughout their known histories. Loya Jirga is just one component of what we know about Jirga. Jirga has operated in the Pukhtoon culture in many horizontal and vertical ways. It is a dispute resolution body at all levels. It has legislative characteristics, plays a diplomatic role, and enjoys many more roles that have rarely been articulated.

We have tried to identify some of the processes of Jirga through describing what Jirga is as well as when, where, why, how, and for whom Jirga works. Our desires are to document various micro processes involved in Jirga, introduce it and its dynamics to those outside of the culture who are dealing with Pukhtoon groups, and to help the Pukhtoons develop Jirga to meet the challenges of present times.

To our understanding, the outside world, with their peculiar worldviews, needs information on Jirga and Pukhtoonwali but find it difficult to agree with what little Pukhtoon worldview offers. The barrier in communication created by the worldview differences is little appreciated particularly by the modern day NGOs and donor community. Rather than discarding an indigenous tradition, the outside world needs to better understand what Pukhtoons have to say, give them confidence to say more, sensitize them to important issues and support them towards education and development. An outright opposition of a deep-rooted culture like Pukhto can contribute little towards developments.

The apparently closed nature of Jirga and its absolute reliance on the Pukhtoon cultural paradigm, the code of Pukhtoonwali, obliges us to explore the Pukhtoon worldview as we talk more about Jirga. While recognizing the danger of overgeneralization, we note that Pukhtoons are typically traditionalists, conservative and devoted to their culture (Pukhtoonwali). Their loyalty to Pukhtoonwali earns them a sense of pride, sometimes leading to ethnocentric attitudes, which outsiders find difficult to understand and accept.

We have tried to present Jirga in its many forms, as is apparent from the table of contents. We would like, however, to provide some initial clarity about our view of Jirga and what it is not. Jirga, in its current form, is not a government or a ruling body. It is not a purely legislative body, nor it is a judicial entity. We see Jirga as a set of processes with similar purposes as many well-known social practices, such as peacebuilding and development. Jirga is operative only in the Pukhtoon areas and its substantive part is governed by the code of Pukhtoonwali.

Because of its roots in Pukhtoonwali, one has to visit the history of Pukhtoons and explore some prominent features of Pukhtoonwali at the outset. Pukhtoonwali is the code under which Jirga finds its jurisdiction and authority. Outside the code, we find that Jirga is a set of processes meant to build communications between parties and people. Beyond this simple capacity of allowing people and parties to talk, Jirga is tied intrinsically to Pukhtoonwali.

A study of Pukhtoonwali will help distinguish between Pukhtoonwali and Jirga. It will also help in finding the links between the two. Through that process we can address the limitations as well as the possibilities of this old system. Along with this, we hope to create space for the Pukhtoons to address some outstanding issues between the Pukhtoon culture and the outside world.

RESEARCHING JIRGA

The complexities involved in describing Jirga can best be understood in the following fable. A few blind persons wanted to see an elephant, but since they were blind, they needed to touch in order to see. Each person got hold of a different part of the elephant and tried to understand how the whole elephant looked. The person who held the leg of the elephant said that an elephant looks like the trunk of a tree. The one who touched the tusk said that the elephant is like a spear. The one who touched the body said that the elephant is like a wall, the one on the tail said that an elephant is like a rope. The descriptions of Jirga are like these found in this story. Our job as researchers has been to sift through the disparate understandings and stories of Jirga and attempt to describe its whole.

This work is an outcome of over two hundred qualitative interviews conducted with a wide range of individuals and groups of Jirga people in formal and informal sessions. Our research spread over about 18 months, during which we traveled extensively in the tribal and settled areas of NWFP and Balochistan in Pakistan, and parts of Afghanistan. Initially we were scheduled to hold only 60 structured interviews with professional Jirga people, but as we advanced our understanding of the different dynamics of Jirga, we got more and more involved in talking to people. Other than the professional Jirga people, we found amazing information in talking to the common people who live under the influence of the Jirga system. We also spoke to a number of people from NGOs and women working on advocacy. The Afghan refugee camps provided us with many resource people from a wide range of areas in Afghanistan.

The methodology of research through qualitative interviews suited our work because, although there are comments and remarks on the Jirga traditions in a number of books written by local as well as foreign writers, to our knowledge, the subject of Jirga has never been a focus of such an extensive study before. We wanted to keep the scope of our work as wide as possible so that future studies on various aspects may commence by interested individuals and groups.

As the title suggests, this work represents an overview of the institution of Jirga, raising some very basic issues and questions. The idea is to simply present the Jirga as it is understood.

There are five basic objectives of the work:

1. To document dynamics of Jirga,
2. To introduce Jirga to the outside world,
3. To look at Jirga as a peacebuilding body,
4. To present Jirga as a grass-roots organization, and
5. To initiate a dialogue regarding the future of Jirga.

The work therefore addresses a wide range of clients including Foreign Governments, Academic Institutions, Non-Governmental Development Organizations and the local population.

The write up provides some patterns of Jirga as defined by our interviewees and seen on the ground. Jirga represents different ideas to different people and, therefore, we have tried to identify each shade of Jirga and each profile of it in very broad terms. This will be helpful for us as we attempt to differentiate between the substantially different forms of Jirga, all of which carry the name of Jirga. On the political side, Jirga is found to be operating at three levels: the national level—more popularly known as Loya Jirga, the regional level, and the local (government) level.

Horizontally, Jirga plays many different roles including those of executive, legislature, and judiciary, all without much distinction in name.

At interpersonal and community levels, Jirga operates as a lubricant for the fragile tribal social setup, binding the Pukhtoons in one social fabric known as Pukhtoonwali. It is very much wrapped up in the meaning Pukhtoons give to their life and it enables them to go on. Jirga's specialization of dispute resolution has been especially highlighted because of the enormous richness and indigenous nature of the processes adopted for peacebuilding.

The work is comprised of the perceptions and understandings of the people regarding their history and the value they attach to it. It also discusses the possible reasons for the special value of this sparsely recorded history. The context of Pukhtoon worldview is further defined through exploring the code of Pukhtoonwali—the basic framework of the Pukhtoon social system.

On our way, an attempt has been made to explore the future prospects for Jirga. We examine the possibilities of using Jirga in the forthcoming local government system, which is under design for the tribal areas of Pakistan. We consider the institutionalization of Jirga at the national level in Afghanistan and also how the development sector can partner with the tribal and rural Jirga.

CHAPTER 1

The Jirga

(Justice Interpreted, Regulated, and Guaranteed Amicably)

"A mass meeting of the elders (of the whole of the Afridi tribe, for instance), would correspond very much to the old `Shiremote' of the Saxon heptarchy; and, indeed, there is more in the simile than one would expect at first glance, for the democratic spirit that is so characteristic a feature in the gradual growth of English customs finds its counterpart in the spirit of liberty and right of free action that is one of the most cherished prerogatives of the Pathan tribesmen, be he ever so humble" (The Hon. Arnold Keppel) [1].

On hearing the word "Jirga", the first question that comes to mind is what is Jirga? There are many different views on the nature and scope of the term Jirga. Most would describe it as an indigenous institution for dispute resolution in the Pukhtoon communities. Yes, it is, but is it more than this as well?

Frozen in the history as the Pukhtoon nation froze, Jirga is an old custom with unmatched potentials for conflict resolution in the Pukhtoon belt of Pakistan and Afghanistan. It is a name given to the model, in which a Pukhtoon society operates, to undertake issues between individuals and between communities, to address concerns, and look for solutions acceptable to all stakeholders.

As a blueprint of Pukhtoon life, Jirga is best summarized as a strategic exchange between two or more people to address an issue through verbal communication. The exchange may or may not result in an agreement on the issue, but the process itself leads the parties, including the interveners, to maintain a certain level of formal communication, thus ensuring peace.

To a common person, Jirga is a body comprised of local, elderly, and influential men in Pukhtoon communities who undertake dispute resolution, primarily through the process of arbitration. Compared to the judicial system of the present day governments, Jirga ensures a fast and cheap justice to the people. Indigenous to Pukhtoon tribal

---

1 www.khyber.org/pashtoculture/pashtoonwalai/jirga.shtml

communities, Jirga is alive even in the areas now influenced by an
Anglo-Saxon legal system and is used for interpersonal dispute
resolution. In the tribal areas, Jirga is the only vehicle through which
the political administration dispenses justice.

According to the modern understanding, Jirga may be noted as an
informal institution as there is little documentation involved, and its
processes are flexible, delicate and little understood by the outside
world. At the same time it is noted that Jirga has enormous impact on
the lives of Pukhtoons, particularly those living in the tribal areas,
mountains or inaccessible areas where government's influence is low.
When seen in practice in those independent areas of Pukhtoon belt,
writers have identified its operation as a reflection of state of liberty
and independence present in the Pushto-speaking world. Author Syed
Abdul Qudus describes it in this way: "The Jirga, by which most
community business, both public and private, are settled in the North
West Frontier Province (and also Balochistan) and Afghanistan, is
probably the closest approach to Athenian democracy that has existed
since times immemorial". Syed Abdul Qudus also relates Jirga to
democracy: "The Jirga represents the essence of democracy in
operation under which every individual[2] has a direct say in shaping the
course of things around him. Practiced this way, democracy operates as
a spiritual and moral force instead of becoming an automation of
votes[3]."

The Jirga is also thought of as a customary judicial institution in which
cases are tried and rewards and punishments inflicted. From the outset,
the use of the Jirga is limited not only to trials of major or minor
crimes and civil disputes, but it also assists in resolving conflicts and
disputes between individuals, groups, and tribes[4].

From these and many other definitions of Jirga, one can see that Jirga
is not only a dispute resolution body, but it has many faces depending
on the purpose and nature of these Jirgas. There is, however, little
distinction in name between these different Jirgas. To Pukhtoons, the
context in which a specific Jirga operates gives a clear and undoubted
understanding of the role and responsibilities of that particular Jirga.

---

2   The word "individual," in this case is being used to refer to men only. In Pukhtoon
     culture, in can be assumed that references to people, community, the public, or the
     individual mean only men and do not include women.

3   www.khyber.org/pashtoculture/Jirga/Jirgas.shtml (by Dr. Mumtaz Bangash)

4   ibid

The only place where distinction is drawn clearly is with the Loya Jirga, a process through which representatives of various areas are organized to discuss and vote on issues at national level.

A common thread for all Jirgas is their operation within an environment of common understanding among the concerned community members. The representatives comprising the Jirga are answerable to the community and cannot afford to betray their trust.

The origins of the Jirga are unclear. Jirga may have been indigenous to the Pukhtoon society or may have come to the area from adjoining Iran[5], but Jirga has helped to enrich the Pukhtoon culture and values. One way it does this is through its influence on the youth. "The discourse among the people in the Jirga is an effective way to teach young ones the real meaning of Pukhtoonwali, the all-encompassing Pukhtoon code of conduct, including Nang and Siali, the codes of honor and social equality"[6].

The operation of Jirga involves a public session where male members of the community gather to deliberate upon an important issue concerning the whole community. There is very little hierarchy evident in its structure. "Sitting in a circle, Jirga has no president, no secretary or convener. There are no hierarchical positions and required status of the participants. All are equal and everyone has the right to speak and argue, although, regard for the elders is always there without any authoritarianism or privileged rights attached to it[7]." In addition, there is no specific quorum for this kind of an assembly. It is expected that the elder members of the Jirga will see that all the stakeholders are duly represented and comments are publicly placed for those missing from the session. People occupy space at random—those more active in public life in the front and those less visible or concerned in public life are at the back. The Jirga system ensures maximum participation of the participants during deliberation of a specific issue as everyone has a right to speak. An issue is examined from point to point till all aspects of the issue are fairly deliberated upon, all concerns heard, and a transparent and uniform understanding of the issue is agreed upon—all the while the Jirga members may keep playing mysteriously with sets of small stones lying before them like a chess board. This apparent

5 Noor ul Amin, an interviewee from Swabi
6 www.khyber.org/pashtoculture/Jirga/Jirgas.shtml (by Dr. Mumtaz Bangash)
7 Ibid

mind mapping (of some of the Jirga members) is said to be one of the techniques to record comments and analyze the situation.

In Afghanistan, a Maraka is a kind of Jirga in which the parties themselves agree to refer the issue to interveners for amicable settlement of the dispute[8]. Literally, Maraka means "opinion" and refers to the opinion of experts sought for clarifying the issues between the parties. Maraka as such does not have any legal or administrative authority to undertake arbitration or other quasi-judicial proceedings. It is a general assembly of people in which important collective issues are discussed, opinions sought, and decisions taken. In case of a conflict involving a murder, parties would go straight for a Jirga rather than Maraka. Maraka is done only with the consent of the parties, initiated by the parties themselves, and only at the preliminary stage of the conflict.

JIRGA PROCESS AND PROCEDURE

Traditional Jirga process is very straightforward and simple in its manner. The Jirga or Maraka is comprised of the 'Spingiris,' or white bearded elder men, and other male members. The 'Spingiris' act as judges and other participants are like jurists. All the parties involved are required to respect the Jirga members. If the parties have any reservation, those need to be shared in the pre-mediation process and stage.

During the Jirga proceedings, all the parties will address the members of the Jirga and not the rival parties directly. Members of the Jirga have a very strong authority to stop parties from speaking if necessary and no offence is taken.

Jirga hears and examines the parties and witnesses to discover the facts of the dispute. Following a thorough discussion with the parties, Jirga members analyze the dispute, keeping in mind the traditional, religious, socio–economic, and geo-political circumstances. After probing inquiries, the Jirga makes every feasible effort to find an unbiased and adequate solution of the problem. The Jirga's pronouncement is usually based on local traditions and /or Shariat[9].

In crucial cases, the Jirga asks parties to clear themselves of the charges by swearing upon the Holy Quraan, which aids in bringing closure to

---

8   In other Pushto speaking parts of Pakistan, use of the term "Maraka" seems less than in Afghanistan.

9   The Code of Islam

the conflict.   At that poi , the dispute stands resolved.   This is prevalent throughout the Pukhtoon region, but its practice and applications varies slightly from area to area.

The Jirga proceedings generally last for a few days depending on the gravity and complexity of the conflict or dispute and the number of parties involved. Jirga endeavors to find an agreeable and acceptable solution to the conflict as early as possible and strives for its enforcement.

DECISION-MAKING AND IMPLEMENTATION

The Jirga or Maraka passes a judgment after necessary investigation into the dispute. No effort is spared to reconcile the disputing parties. The decisions are of two types, Haq or the right, and Waak, which means authority, and both sides are allowed to present their arguments before a decision is given.

In case of Haq, each party has the right to challenge the decision of the Jirga on its merit. If one of the parties is not satisfied with the verdict and feels that the Jirga has not done justice, they can quote precedents and rules (Narkh) to plead their point and reject the decision. It is interesting that different tribes may have different Narkh in similar cases. In the case of Haq, the aggrieved party has the right to bring another Maraka or Jirga to re-examine the issue. In doing so, the decision given on the third occasion is usually considered final.

In the case of Waak, the two parties repose their full confidence in the Jirga and authorize it to decide the case according to its best judgment. The parties have to abide by the decision and cannot challenge it. The decision the Jirga members reach, however, is unanimous.

In most situations, Jirga seeks to obtain approval of the parties before announcing a verdict, even in arbitration cases. Implementation of a Jirga decision is crucial to the credibility of Jirga. When the decision seems reasonable to both the parties, it can be effectively implemented; however, when one of the parties has serious objections to the outcome of the Jirga, the implementation process becomes difficult, if not impossible.

Anyone who then does not abide by the decision of the Jirga is subject to punitive measures. The Jirga determines the type of punishment based on Narkh (tribal rule, or precedent). This practice varies from one part of the tribal areas to another. Anyone who rejects collective wisdom takes a grave risk—a Jirga can impose powerful sanctions to

enforce its judgment. The sanctions can include ex-communication of
the non-compliant person or group.

Additional punishments can include the confiscation of rifles belonging
to the non-compliant party, placing them with the Jirga as 'Gravey'
(bond or guarantee). The Jirga can also impose heavy fines for the
non-compliant party to pay to the complying party in the dispute. If
non-compliance persists, the Jirga can use force by sending men to
burn down the party's house(s). If someone still remains defiant and
does not comply with the Jirgas orders, he is considered to be
'Kabarjan', the arrogant one. By doing so, he loses the security
promised by the Jirga, and thus may be killed by his opponents
without any consequence.

A council of the tribesmen (under different names) implements the
collective decisions of Qaumi or Ulusi Jirgas (see the description in the
next section): these are the Salwaikhtee (40's) in Waziristan, the
Lashkar in Afridi areas, and the Rapakian in Kurram Agency.
Typically, this body is comprised of about forty members and its
effectiveness is determined by the strength and sanctions they derive
from the tribal people, whom they volunteer to serve.

The practice of Jirga is not uniform throughout the Pukhtoon belt,
however, the above description relates to a fairly ideal form of practice
prevalent in most parts of the Pukhtoon belt where Jirga dominates the
lives of its people without any external influences. Where there is some
form of governmental system in place, the processes of Jirga and its
credibility will vary. Nevertheless, the people of the Pushto speaking
world place enormous confidence in Jirga.

Jirga operates within a context. Outside of that context, Jirga would
be impossible. The context of Jirga is based on a shared understanding
of history, values, traditions, culture, local environment, and above all
the Pushto language. These local practices are more popularly known
as "Pukhtoonwali", the code of Pukhtoon life!

The Pukhtoon worldview represents a group of proud people who
have a visible cliché to relate their history and past practices of their
forefathers and to draw deductions for their future course. In the
coming chapters we will review various aspects of Pukhtoon history
and traditions to find out the context in which Jirga operates.
Subsequently we will try to explore more aspects of Jirga. The
relationship between Jirga and the Pukhtoon culture and their
interdependence or otherwise, will remain the focus of our study.

CHAPTER 2

The Context of Jirga

There are more mysteries about Pukhtoon culture than Jirga.

(Noorul Amin)

Jirga operates within the context of Pukhtoonwali, outside of which it could not function. The popular proverb of "doing Pukhto" implies that all actions taken (by a person or a group) are in conformity with the broader code of Pukhtoonwali or Pukhtoon culture. Sometimes it is asserted that a person doesn't even need to speak Pushto to be a real Pathan[10], implying that the code of Pukhtoonwali is merely associated with a set of traits and characteristics. A person would only need to exercise those in order to be recognized as a real Pukhtoon. However, use of the Pushto language and the shared history draw the circumference in which the insider-insider communication on what is Pukhtoonwali and what it is not takes place. A full explanation of Pukhtoonwali is neither simple nor possible. Despite the belief of locals about the universal nature of Pukhtoonwali, social practices vary from place to place. However, we will try to capture some of the striking features of the code of Pukhtoonwali, particularly those related to conflict and peacebuilding, such that we may find answers to the "whys" of the practice of Jirga.

The practice of Jirga is so deeply entwined with Pukhtoonwali that it is difficult to imagine Jirga outside of this context. Similarly, the context of Pukhtoonwali is deeply dependant upon the common history of conformity to the code of Pukhtoonwali.

We will go though the general overview of the history and some popular traits of Pukhtoonwali so that we are able to understand the Pukhtoon worldview. At that point we will have set the foundation for exploring Jirga, a practice inherently influenced by Pukhtoonwali.

PUKHTOONS OR PATHANS

(pᵊtänz´), a group of semi-nomadic peoples consisting of more than 60 tribes, numbering approximately 10 million in Pakistan and 6

---

10   "George Ka Pakistan", TV show on GeoTV, George a British national, meeting Jirga head in Afridi area, aired January 2005

million (43%) in Afghanistan, where they form the dominant ethnic group (historically known as Afghans and now typically as Pukhtoons). Pathans are Muslims and speak Pashto (or Pushto). They are also known as Pashtuns, Pushtuns, Pukhtoons, and Pakhtoons[11] titled with a general suffix as "Khan", although many Pukhtoons prefer to write a reference to their immediate clan, group, or tribe as well.

In this chapter, we will give a general description of a people of deep ethnocentricity, who strongly identify themselves as Pukhtoons. The information provided here is rooted in the popular belief system of this creed of people. Pukhtoons take pride in who they are and find good reasons for that deep pride or arrogance. It is a source of inspiration for them to display dignity and character; a phenomenon that Pukhtoons believe is diminishing in the modern material world.

"Though the origin of Pukhtoons is unclear, legends say that they are the descendants of Afghana, grandson of King Saul. Most scholars, however, believe that the Pukhtoons probably arose from the hundreds of years of intermingling of ancient invaders in the regions now comprising Afghanistan. Pukhtoons resemble Caucasians, are of medium height, with strong, straight noses, black hair, and dark eyes, although there is high prevalence of blue, green, and gray eyes"[12].

Although their dialect may change from place to place, in the present day, Pukhtoons are an ethnic group of people sharing a single language known as Pukhto. Variation between the accent and dialect can be as drastic as between the people belonging to Quetta and Peshawar. Someone from one region will find difficulty in understanding the language of the other, as the words are drastically different, but still, they share the same grammar. Some regions have an influence of the neighboring Persian language as well. There are, however, two versions of written Pushto that are slightly different from each other. One is of the Peshawar region and the other of Afghanistan. Most poetry and literature in Pakistan is found in Peshawar script, being more influenced by the Neighboring Indian Urdu, whereas the Afghan script is slightly different.

Besides the "Pukhto", the common cultural traits, Pukhtoons identify each other by two main factors. Firstly, the caste or the last name, and secondly, the place of living or dwelling, such as Swat or Buner. It is

---

[11] www.cia.gov/cia/publications/factbook/docs/profileguide.html
[12] www.pakhtun.com/Aboutpakhtuns.htm

generally believed that the earlier nomads who gradually settled in different places made clusters of their families. These are thought of as the first inhabitants of the region. These families came to be known as specific clans whose generations followed the name of their ancestors. No one would know more about his or her origin than the fact that he is a Yousufzai or a Khattak. Yousufzai, being a larger tribe, has innumerable sub casts, similar to other tribes. Therefore, a person may introduce himself as "Mandharr" and yet he would also be a Yousufzai. Within the village or neighborhood, this sub cast again would divide in khails like Jogi Khail, Khan Khail, and so on, to the lowest tier of identity, all being proud Pukhtoons.

With the support of simplistic theories, people also identify themselves with areas and regions. A person belonging to the Karak district of NWFP will generally be expected to be a "Khattak." If not, without much concern with the age and time, the person would have an explanation as to how his ancestors reached this area.

Unwritten as it is, a detailed examination of these two factors, the area and the clan or caste definitely gives an idea of how families and tribes might have moved from west (Afghanistan) to East (Pakistan).

THEORIES OF PUKHTOON HISTORY

Pukhtoon history can be divided into three main phases:

Pre-Historic Times

Without deeply referencing theories of archeology, the first phase of history comprises of those beliefs that begin the narration from the pre-historic times when people lived in the caves and mountains, usually as nomads. There is no documented record of those times, but the general understanding is that people lived a remote life in the mountains of Hindukush. There is also no proof that these people spoke the Pushto language.

Middle Ages

The second layer of history moves from Alexander's time to the Islamic times when either the people from Afghanistan were linked to Arabia or they tried to establish some link with them. Contrary theories negate this notion of a Jirga meeting the Prophet Mohammad (Peace Be Unto Him) as better records indicate that the people in Afghanistan were still Buddhists until a few hundred years after the introduction of Islam.

Historian Niamat Ullah says that the lack of authentic books on Pukhtoon history is due to the fact that the Prophet Musa (Moses) surpassed Pharaoh and took Jerusalem and Syria[13]. Then Bakht-e-Nasr attacked Israelis, captured all their lands, looted Jerusalem, and exiled them from their country. The Israelis became gypsies, moving from one place to another and permanently settled nowhere. They lacked literate as well as religious activities, and if they had any activity those were relinquished gradually. They did not have means to record the events of their present and recent past.

Present Times

The third phase of the history of Pukhtoons is the most recent and the most credible one. This can go as back as far as the 17th century, but better records are available for the eighteenth century and beyond when the Russians and British were engaged in "The Great Game[14]." There are plenty of books written and available from western authors regarding the geography, traditions, and culture of these Pukhtoons and Afghans as the British, as well as the Russians, tried to explore the area and understand its people. Western scholars took keen interest in the Pukhtoon culture and traditions as people followed quite sophisticated, indigenous, and autonomous life style, which were difficult to handle through the regular imperial methods of Russia and the British.

The Jewish Link

Most local historians link the larger Pukhtoon tribe with the twelve tribes of Jews, who are said to be expelled from Jerusalem by the invading Bakhte-Nasr (598 BC)[15]. One of those tribes found abode in the present day Afghanistan, which is believed to be named after the grandfather of these tribes, namely "Afghana". Some historians are of the opinion that "Afghana" was the son of the Prophet Ismail and grandson of the Prophet Ibrahim (Abraham). Others argue that Afghana was the son of Armiya and Armiya was the son of the Prophet

---

[13] Ataullah Khan, Qazi, The Pukhtano Tareekh (Pukhtoon History), Idara Ishaate Sarhad, Peshawar, p 12

[14] Peter Hopkirk's The Great Game

[15] Hafiz Mohammad Ishaq, "Yahood-o-Nasara Quraan Ki Nazar Main", page 402

Taloot. While confirming the Jewish nature, some historians also narrate the story that when Nadir Shah (of Iran) attacked the Indian subcontinent and reached Peshawar, the elders of Yousufzai tribe presented the invaders with a copy of Torah in the Hebrew language along with many other things used by the Jews in their worship. The Jews in Nadir Shah's army recognized those things and identified these people as Jews. Abdullah Khan Hirati, a Pukhtoon historian, is of the opinion that the Prophet Taloot was the king of Jews, who had two sons, one was Afghan and the other was Jaloot. Afghan was the grandfather of the Pukhtoon tribe and that is why Pukhtoons are also called Afghans"[16].

The Islamic Link

These tribes followed Jewish religion until the inception of Islam. Khalid bin Waleed, a companion of the Prophet Mohammad (PBUH), is believed to be from this tribe. It is believed that Khalid Bin Waleed sent a message to his relatives residing in the mountains of "Ghore[17]" to embrace Islam. These people in turn sent a delegation (Jirga) to Makkah / Madina under the leadership of one Qais to inquire about the teachings of Islam. Upon meeting with the Prophet Mohammad (PBUH) and being impressed with his teachings, all of them became Muslim. On their way back, a few Arab preachers of Islam accompanied them to Afghana for extending the teachings of Islam to others. In about the next forty years or so, it is believed that all these tribes in Afghana area converted to Islam.

Some historians are of the opinion that when the Arabs conquered this region, they gave this name (Afghan) to Pukhtoons due to their chatter behavior among themselves and during their Jirgas. The word afghan has been derived from Arabic language, which means chattering. "If the origin of a race can be determined on the basis of customs and traditions then Pukhtoon would be closer to Arabs. The study of Arabian and Pukhtoon society presents a remarkable resemblance particularly in their tribal organization and social usages. Both possess the same virtues and characteristics"[18].

---

16   Ataullah Khan, Qazi, The Pukhtano Tareekh (Pukhtoon History), Idara Ishaate Sarhad, Peshawar, (Extracts from)
17   A mountain in Afghanistan
18   Azim Afridi, Monthly Diplomat,
      http://www.geocities.com/pashtow/pukhtun_history.htm

The significance of history to Pukhtoons as a people is quite interesting in the cultural context, but there is no resolution of the discussion as to whether Pukhtoons are descendants of Bani Israel or of someone else. Perhaps this nostalgia is associated with the Pukhtoons pride of being a martial race. For the purpose of this work, we tend to agree that Pukhtoons, with reference to their history, try to represent in their culture and conduct a level of prudence that distinguishes them from others in the region.

SOCIAL HIERARCHIES

As the argument goes, Pukhtoons are one of the largest ethnic groups of the world today[19]. Despite the difference in dialects, areas and castes, Pukhtoon homogeneity is ensured by their common culture, the code of Pukhtoonwali. This culture somehow remains above the scrutiny of religion as well, although loyalty to Islam resides as an integral factor of pride for Pukhtoons. Interestingly enough, Pukhtoons form a homogeneous group of people, rich and poor, educated and illiterate, mountainous and residents of plain areas, where all are equal Pukhtoons, each individual fully independent in his own right, and all are ideally integrated into the larger fabric of the society.

Known for its highly egalitarian nature, Pukhtoons often debate if their societies are hierarchical or not. History tells that Pukhtoons liked to class themselves as Pukhtoons only, but allowed professional classes, like the ironsmith, the carpenters, the clergy, and the shoemakers as part of their social tenancies. These professional groups, despite their second grade status, were assured liberties and freedoms available to rest of the society but were not allowed to call themselves Pukhtoons. Today the distinction is less and less visible as the societies are integrating faster than the past, while continuously attempting to conform to the code of Pukhtoonwali, or Pukhto.

An element of feudal structure can also be seen here and there as a few families found fortunes at different times in the history[20]. Even these Khans and Nawabs had to adjust to the somewhat independent nature of Pukhtoons.

Pukhtoons have a strong male-dominated system in which women stay in veils, in the four walls, behind the curtains, and in the backdrop.

---

[19] www.pakhtun.com/aboutpakhtun.htm

[20] Northern NWFP houses popular Nawab families, including Nawab of Dir, Nawab of Bajaur & Khans/Waali of Swat etc.

Although in the rural areas women engage extensively in agriculture and cattle's breeding, as well as child rearing and other household activities, their labor is unpaid in cash. In the urban areas and among well off families, women stay at home, raise their children, and look after the kitchen affairs.

Under a plea of special sanctity provided by religion as well as traditions, all social, political, and economic affairs of the family and the society are lead by men. Talking to men about women brings a feeling of shyness, and cultural respect prevents people from talking about women. A sarcastic remark about one's wife, mother, sister, or daughter can lead to a high degree of ferocity: a legitimate reason to get violent. This segregation between men and women also breeds a special culture of female groups in which women enjoy a certain level of autonomy in various social activities like arranging marriages or exchanging pleasantries between families.

Men do agree to engage in consultation with women on major decisions of life such as issues of the household, children, and even decisions about external business. Most men deny being influenced by such consultations. Interestingly, there are examples of women leading political parties[21] and involved in regular work in government, NGOs and other commercial setups. In Afghanistan too, the cultural setting of urban areas like Kabul provide much more space to women as compared to the rural and remote areas, where people see urban culture with quite some contempt for allowing female entry to public life.

The patriarchal system extends into the practice of Jirga where currently women do not have the precedent of participation, although Bushra Gohar, a renowned social worker and activist says that in the past women did participate in the proceedings of Jirgas.

---

21 Mrs. Naseem Wali Khan as leader and president of ANP, a nationalist political party

THE PUKHTOONS .

"Pukhtoons insist that being a "real Pukhtoon" demands that one not just speak Pukhto, but "do Pukhto," that is, follow the precepts of the Pukhtoonwali[22]."

The word Pukhtoon is sometimes believed to be abbreviated from a set of traits known to be associated with Pukhtoons as a people: "P" for Patt or Family Honor, "Kh" for Khaigara means Compassion, "T" Toora or Triumph, "W" for Wafa means loyalty and "N" for Nang or Pride

Traditionally settlers and nomads of the Hindukush and Kohi-Suleman ranges, Pukhtoons are now spread all over present day Afghanistan, some parts of Pakistan, and all over the Indian subcontinent. Many Pukhtoons reside in cities including Kabul, Jalalabad, Herat, Peshawar, and Quetta.

The Government of NWFP and Balochistan, which include the two provinces of Pakistan and the Central Government of Afghanistan, are represented by this creed of people called Pukhtoons, who have a state of mind different and distinctive in its own right.

Deeply committed to their non-religious and some times irreligious traditional practices, Pukhtoons are also naively dedicated to Islam. This contrast of their belief system and its actual practice is reiterated when religion is taken as a part of traditional values, rather than subjecting historical traditions to the scrutiny of Islamic teachings.

CULTURE OF PUKHTOONS

"I despise the man who does not guide his life by honor; the very word honor drives me nuts."   (Khushal Khan Khattak)[23]

Distinctive tribal customs and traditions are an integral part of the Pukhtoon society. Pukhtoon cultural values are reflected in a code of ethics called simply Pukhto and Pukhtoonwali (the way of the Pukhtoon).

A combination of conventions, traditions, and a code of honor known as "Pukhtoonwali" govern the social system of Pukhtoons. Through

---

[22] Thomas .J. Barifield, Afghan Customary Law and Its Relationship to Formal Judicial Institutions, Boston University, Produced for the United States Institute for Peace, Washington, DC, June 26, 2003

[23] www.khyber.org/pashtoculture.shtml

this unwritten code, the basic thread of the Pukhtoons' social fabric, Pukhtoon soc: es around the region lead a diverse and yet dynamic way of life.

Any argument that doesn't make sense in a particular situation can be conveniently challenged as non-Pukhto, thereby insisting that Pukhto, the culture of Pukhtoons is highly sensible and is equally sensitive to logic. The most common argument is that of holding onto old traditions, whether right or wrong. This flux between advancement under logic and restrai it under fear exercises a great influence on the actions of Pukhtoons and has been held sacred by them for generations.

It is believed that Pukhtoonwali or the Pukhtoon code of honor embraces all the activities from the cradle to the grave. Besides many micro-social practices, the Pukhtoonwali imposes a few additional obligations upon the members of Pukhtoon society, which are explained in the following paragraphs.

Hujra

As old as perhaps the Jirga itself is, Hujra is a community club situated in each village, each Khail (street) and some times owned by a well off family but shared by the whole community. Other than a place to accommodate collective ceremonies, male members of the community who hang out and associate like a larger family regularly attend hujra(s). Members of a Hujra are mostly close relatives but other people from neighborhood are also welcomed. Elderly people spend their day to enjoy hubble-bubble and chat over the tea, younger men in their spare time listen to the stories of elders and raise issues while the children keep playing around, waiting for a call from one of the elders to take a message or bring fresh tea. A guest house for male guests, Hujra also serves as a place to initiate Jirgas. Issues are put on the table, brainstormed and a consensus is developed before the issue can be put to the wider community. Hujra is considered to be a secular place but closely associated with Hujra is the role of mosque in the neighborhood. Although there are few similarities between a mosque and a Hujra, the role of mosque has gained more importance recently due to many national and regional settings tilted towards Islamization. Additionally, the role of Hujra is diminishing from community life because of the economic trends, and a faster pace of life which allows little leisure time with people to spare for community based activities.

Decay in the institution of Hujra is definitely affecting the efficacy of Jirga, but this study tends not necessarily to argue for reinvigoration of Hujra; rather our focus will remain to find strengths and challenges for Jirga from where it is today and move forward.

Nanawatay

Nanawatay means repentance over past hostility or inimical attitudes and the granting of asylum. Walking down to someone under Nanawatay means having an expression or attitude of submission—a combination of humility, sorrow, and apology—and giving space to the other person to respond with "grace", so precious to Pukhto. A party or a person wanting to apologize to another does Nanawatay. Nanawatay is thus responded to through granting asylum. Asylum implies security from the wrath of others. An expression of Nanawatay would simply oblige the other party to put aside the anger and pain so suffered during an unpleasant interaction, at least temporarily, and treat the other party with all Pukhtoon sensibilities. This creates space for a peaceful dialogue, a medium of communication not available under strained relationships. It is not obligatory to agree to a pardon in all cases under a Nanawatay, however, in most cases, a Nanawatay would mean restoration of honor for both parties. Depending on how deeply the other person might be hurt, a Nanawatay once offered can be repeated through different methods in a particular case. Taking along a goat as a gift, laying down one's headgear, handing over a weapon, taking one's own women and children to the opposite party are all expressions of Nanawatay. Similarly, acknowledgement of Nanawatay by the receiving party is an element of the grace embodied within Pukhto. The party may demand a more public apology, a more appropriate respite, or a more suitable restitution, but a Nanawatay once done is duly counted towards fulfilling a major obligation of Pukhto and asylum is a natural outcome of such pro-activity.

Teega[24]

Teega, defined as a truce, is declared by the parties or by the society and is represented by a Jirga in order to avoid further bloodshed between two rival factions. Symbolized with marking of a stone, Teega represents a ground rule and defines transition from violence to

---

24   Teega is sometimes also called Machalga.

peaceful negotiations between the parties. It embodies the consent of the communities and is used as a reference for the resolution of future disputes. This is also used to establish the ground rules for conduct between two or more tribes, so it takes the shape of a treaty and is tagged with specific penalties for violation. For a public issue, like the banning of aerial firing on festivals, Teega can be announced unilaterally by the society. When it is announced for warring factions, Jirga has to consult the parties, recognize their differences, analyze the situation, and impose a ban on specific activities by the parties so that more sensible options are explored. Teega, a ban on further activities of the nature, ensures the security of the lives of the warring parties and is respected by the parties in their allegiance to the larger system of Pukhto. A Teega is extended where there remain difficulties unresolved between the parties during the first period of Teega. Violation of a Teega can result in imposition of a fine on the violating party and/ or allowing the other to resort to a fiercer offensive. It is also a socially condemnable phenomenon in which the violator party is charged for nonconfirmity to their words.

In some places specific names are given to such instruments of social control. Tarr and Bandarr[25] are used for community-imposed restrictions to suit their collective environment.

Melmastiya

Openhearted hospitality, or Melmastiya, is one of the most cherished features of Pukhto. It is closely associated with the notion of asylum, as someone seeking hospitality is considered equal to someone invited by the host. Hospitality means not only the service of food and other needs, it also means automatic assurance of an environment of security and peace prevalent in the host's household. There is quite some symbolism attached with the phenomenon of hospitality. When Pukhtoons are asked to name their social traits that distinguish them from other societies and cultures, hospitality takes number one. This level pride and its articulation leave little room for doubts on the intent of what Pukhtoons mean by Hospitality. Pukhtoon worldview in respect of hospitality also came to limelight when negotiations regarding handing over of Osama Bin Laden to US were going on

---

25 Local terms

between USA and Taliban government in Afghanistan. Afghanistan's refusal to hand over Osama to the US is said to be attributed to the point that Osama was seen a guest whose handing over to US would speak negative on the identity of Afghans.

The trait of hospitality is guarded by Pukhtoons on two grounds. Firstly, it is strongly promoted by Islam. Secondly, it is argued that hospitality is a traditional and cultural etho. Most of our interviewees justified the institution of hospitality first on the historical basis and later took support of religion to substantiate their argument. Nevertheless, the sanctity associated with the phrase of hospitality is all encompassing.

Paighaur

Paighaur, or taunt, is yet another recognized perspective of Pukhtoon behavior. A sarcastic remark by peers can drive a person blindly to follow the tenants of Pukhtoonwali, leading to violence and bloodshed. Apprehension of possible Paighaur can generate internal social controls on people limiting their actions and forcing them to conform to the ethics of Pukhtoonwali. This also helps people maintain a character worthy of a good Pukhtoon. As such, a Paighaur can come from one's own relative, like a father or mother, or even a friend, and the person receiving a Paighaur is not blamed much for the upcoming violence as a result of this instigation. Paighaur on a women or public talk about women can cause trouble for the proud Pukhtoon man.

Peace

One distinctive characteristic of Pukhtoonwali is the idea of peace and its propagation. As a virtue not only suggested by religion, Pukhtoonwali dictates its leadership to preach for peace under all circumstances. This ideal of peace leads the Jirga to gauge the corollaries of justice in an artistic way. Where ennity and revenge are the personal concerns of individuals and families; moving towards peace is the professional obligation of every elder under Pukhtoonwali. The Jirga is built on the rhetoric of peace and strives to always advance in the path of peace and peacebuilding. Due to the repeated and numerous examples of violent conflicts within Pukhtoon communities, Jirga has a sure case to plead for peace.

INSTITUTIONS /ELEMENTS OF CONFLICT IN PUKHTOON SOCIETY

Various cultural traits, traditions, habits, and narratives which form the code of Pukhtoons are called Pukhto or Pukhtoonwali. Conformity to Pukhto is a sign of a level playing field for all and also gives Pukhtoons a sense of confidence in their culture and traditions. These elements of Pukhtoon life may look strange to outsiders but they are a reality, practiced and sustained by this group of people who are unwilling to change. Some important elements and institutions of Pukhtoonwali are related to conflict and violence, as explained below.

Enmity or Dushmani

Pukhtoons may be one of the few cultures in the world today that cherish maintaining a rivalry with their relatives, neighbors, or even first cousins. Sources of enmity or the root causes of the rivalry can be many, but the fact that enmity has been declared as an institution, announced by one, or imposed upon the other, binds the two groups in a different kind of relationship. This relationship gives each other the right to kill, according to rules well known and understood by all.

The family maintaining an enmity will take due precautions to secure their lives from an ambush, an assault, or a shabkhoon[26] (blitz). Fort-like houses are maintained in the tribal areas with watchtowers on all corners from which random aerial firing is done every night to prevent any possible surprise attack.

Under enmity, a family may wait for years to take revenge for an earlier killing. Young children are inculcated to take revenge for the killing of their father or uncle when they grow up. In this way, the enmity, silent for sometimes decades, may cause a sudden assault by one party on the other, giving new life to the institution of enmity. The judicial and court processes, if any, may proceed according to needs of the time, but the personal, one for one equation remains a factor of wrestling between the two groups.

Tarbourwali, or First Cousin Hood

The element of extreme jealousy among first cousins on the paternal side is recognized as a natural consequence of the relationship. Many

---

[26] A night attack to burn the enemies house and kill all the male members

reasons are cited for this attitude of jealousy, but the most suspected is perhaps the distribution of property among the heirs of real brothers. Joint family living and the use of different degrees of sharing of the family resources, or fast accomplishments by one family as compared to the others, might be visible in a situation of acute Tarbourwali.

Most of the time, at a marginal threshold of bloodshed, Tarbourwali can transform into a full-fledged enmity to be carried forward to the next generations of the same cousins. The same Tarbourwali is also quickly forgotten in the face of an external enemy. The family fights the outsider as a unit.

Revenge and Homicide

The term used for revenge is called "Badal," or exchange. Badal can be a positive return or reply as well as negative, such as an obligation to seek revenge by retaliation. This retaliation can be immediate but it is generally a well-considered calculation of counting kills. Two men killed from each side would create enough common ground to initiate a dialogue for ending the conflict, as there is nothing else on which to settle the score. However, living with an imbalanced score is a life long shame for the immediate male relative of the victim, more than for the rest of his family. Even young children are groomed to wait for an appropriate day to take revenge. Again, the person taking the revenge does not go beyond what is equal to their family's right (earlier loss), and lives a life of total satisfaction and due Pukhtoon pride thereafter. Revenge can trigger counter revenge, but enmity is a phenomenon worth living in the Pukhtoon society.

Closely associated with the phenomenon of enmity, revenge is considered a way of achieving justice; it is not a privilege but a right and duty of a Pukhtoon. As part of the phenomenon of enmity, root causes of the conflict may be long forgotten, but the opposite party would give priority to the task of taking care of the most recent offence. Although the term revenge could be used in a "tit for tat" sense for each malicious action of one party against the other, it is generally associated with the act of murder only. Murder can be divided in a few different categories:

A murder in innocence: This refers to an accidental killing where a person may be killed in crossfire between two other parties or in a road accident. When the heirs are satisfied that the killing was accidental, only a head money or a public apology (followed by a Nanawatay) is sufficient to settle the dispute. Most such killings are received as the will of God.

A murder with malice: In this case, a person may be suspected of having killed someone with malicious intentions. The heirs of such a victim are therefore obliged to kill the murderer or one of his male relatives. This may give birth to a series of revenge killings, unless the murderer party approaches the victim party with an appropriate apology including compensation, fixed according to the local law. This may include cash money and/or transfer of girls in marriage[27] from the offender party to the victim party. When it is difficult to prove whether the event occurred accidentally or whether there was some malice involved, onus of providing such proof lies with the party under suspicion of murder. The victim party can only observe the things silently, and if convinced of malice by the other party, a revenge of appropriate nature[28] should follow.

Murder under enmity: Under a pre-declared enmity, killing counts just towards the scores of the parties, reducing the number of male representatives of the opponent family and pressurizing them to reach an imbalanced compromise with the offender party. A compromise under such coercion does not mean a settlement, but recognition of reality by the weaker party and supremacy by the offender party. While the offender party would continue to take precautions from public encounter with the victim party, such enmity may thus stay in abeyance for ten, twenty, or thirty years before a boy from the victim party grows up to complete the revenge of his elders killed earlier.

Honor Killing: In contrast to the three types of murders defined above, the concept of honor killing emanates from practices of illicit sex, adultery, or sometimes even rape. The community, or more specifically the father or brothers of the girl and the boy, are obliged to kill their respective offspring involved in illicit sex. In some cases, however, the community can allow the escape, or forced exile

---

27   The tradition of Swara is a hot issue with international advocacy and women's rights groups. To locals, giving a girl in marriage should serve two purposes: it provides a replacement for the life lost and binds the two families in a marital alliance that should act as a barrier against further hostilities.

28   A state of half-declared enmity where a mysterious accident involving one party could follow with an equally mysterious murder from the other side.

(Kashunda), of the boy from the area. This saves the life of the girl in some cases and allows the girl's parents to kill the boy, instead, if he is ever found in the vicinity. Nature of proof of illicit relationship may vary from place to place and situation to situation. Even an approach for intimacy by a boy may call for the killing of such a boy by the guardians of the girl for harming their honor. Sometimes, under strict influence of Pukhtoonwali, even father of the boy might choose to kill his own son for dishonoring the family. There have also been instances of women killing their husbands for keeping illicit relations with another woman.

SOCIAL SENSITIVITIES

Pukhtoon society binds its members to a number of unique and sometimes senseless sets of practices. To understand the Pukhtoon worldview it will be helpful to go through the set of rules that form the larger understanding of life in Pukhtoon societies.

Theft

In the absence of state authorities, issues that involve trespassing or property theft entail both risks to the thief as well as to the victim of theft. In the settled and agricultural areas, cattle theft or stealing may be more common than in the tribal or mountainous areas where people are generally well prepared to shoot and kill in self-defense, making it more dangerous for the thief to trespass. As the result of a theft, a family should feel dishonored, as they may be perceived as too weak or cowardly to protect themselves. Such a perception insults not only their honor but also may invite more thefts. If the victim knows the identity of a thief, the accused can be required to take an oath as part of Jirga proceedings. The accused must either prove his innocence or admit to the theft and make amends.

The word Bilga is used for stolen property. According to tribal custom, a man is held responsible for a dacoity, a theft or burglary, if any of the stolen articles are recovered from his house, unless the source of such stolen property is disclosed to the community.

Oath

Aspects of the oath also deserve a mention here. Generally, to Pukhtoons, an oath based on religion is quite meaningful and also rarely done. Once a man takes an oath it is determined that he is free of guilt. However, the party making the accusation may still not be satisfied with such oath. In this case, the party may demand that the man take an oath on his wife. An oath on one's wife entails that the husband must take an honest oath or their marriage will dissolve in the spiritual sense. Sanctity and symbolism attached to the wife is so deep and precious that, in many cases, men who took an oath on God later confessed to the crime when asked to take an oath on wife. Taking an oath has two forms: a person may be required to take an oath, or someone may "throw" an oath on the accused party. The person upon whom such an oath is thrown is expected to be as honest as if he were taking an oath voluntarily.

Sex

Sexual misbehavior is subject to rigorous consequences because it is deemed an offence against family honor. Adultery is punished by killing both individuals if they are caught in bed together. If only one of the two is slain, the killing is viewed as illegitimate because it throws suspicion on the killer's motives. In the case of forcible rape or if a woman reports that she has been sexually harassed, only the man is liable to be killed. While sexual crimes are primarily committed by men on women, adolescent boys and girls also fall victim.

Such honor killings may also occur in cases of elopement (or forcible abduction) when an unmarried girl runs off with a man without her family's permission. Because her father and brothers are then expected to kill them, the couple often flees the area and seeks sanctuary (Nanawatay) elsewhere. They may later try to regularize their status by providing indemnity (pour), a shame payment. The man's family must also provide a woman or two in marriage (Swara) to the offended family by way of apology.

Declaration of 'Tor' literally means guilty. A person may be declared a black-sheep by the community for his or her illicit and illegitimate approach to another partner. It is an ancient tradition, prevalent in neighboring cultures[29] as well. The cases of adultery and illicit relations are put down with an iron hand and no mercy is shown to the culprits, neither male nor female.

---

[29]   Karo kari in Sindh

There is ample evidence of the presence of adultery and homosexuality in some segments of Pukhtoon society. It is thought within the Pukhtoon culture that the severity of punishment will act as a deterrent for such inappropriate behavior; however, the very fact that these harsh punishments are awarded is the testimony to the argument that it is a natural tendency of human beings to form these kinds of relationships. In this way, Pukhtoons are no different from other societies and cultures where such behavior also exists.

In cases of the abduction of a married woman, the woman and her lover are similarly liable to be killed if caught by either the husband's family or the woman's family since both have had their honor offended. Such abduction may therefore lead to the emergence of a difficult and long-lasting blood feud.

Family Laws

In Pukhtoon society, most marriages are arranged. They often involve long negotiations and questions may arise as to when or if a commitment is binding. Negotiations center first on whether the offer of marriage should be accepted. Vulvur or Walwar, which is the price to be paid by the groom's family to the bride's parents, is practiced in some areas.

Although by religious law divorce is relatively easy for a man to declare, among Pukhtoons divorce itself is viewed as dishonorable and, therefore, rare. Under Islamic law, a man can have up to four wives. Although it is practiced rarely, polygamy is socially allowed only for the need of offspring, particularly a boy.

Pairs of children are sometimes announced engaged by the elderly women or the family heads when the children are still infants. Despite the medical opinion that marriages among close relatives have the risk of congenital defects in offspring, the practice of consanguineous marriages, particularly with first cousins, is a common phenomenon. In some cases, young children may even be married prior to puberty.

Another area of trouble is a forcible engagement (ghazh) in which a man publicly announces his engagement to a girl, making it difficult for anyone else to propose to the girl. The parents of the girl either have to kill such a volunteer groom, or to avoid such nonsense; they can ignore the announcement and arrange a marriage of their daughter in some other village. It is also possible to reconcile with the announcement and agree to the marriage. Settlement after such a humiliating announcement by a social deviant demands high profile Nanawatay and tough negotiations from girl's parents, including the demand of an exchange marriage of a girl or two from the boy's family.

Property

Three basic disputes commonly arise over land based on:
1) Questions of ownership and the right to sell
2) Water rights
3) Encroachments by neighbors on personal and community property

Land records are generally not maintained in the Pukhtoon areas because there has never been effective presence of the government. Secondly, there is little culture of maintaining and trusting the written system. An owner of private agricultural land has the right to sell or mortgage it for a loan. However, determining who has the legal right to sell or pledge such land may be disputed. Partitioning of land is considered a weak gesture in Pukhtoonwali, which encourages people to continue to live in a joint family system. Unfortunately, Pukhtoonwali does not prescribe any method of partitioning lands between the heirs. It also does not prescribe a reasonable mechanism for a family unit that wishes to split from the joint family. Subfamilies within the larger joint family may begin to use common lands or other property, allowing a disproportional share in the property to the heirs who might deserve more. The more the family delays the partition, the more complex the matter might get, eventually leading to complex misunderstandings between first cousins. Demand of early partition is also strongly resisted by those holding the possession of such lands, thus making the issue more difficult.

Rights to land usually involve rights to water as well because irrigation is what makes productive agriculture possible. Questions of water cycle and the maintaining of irrigation channels through community work are sorted out at the village level through the community Jirga system.

An offence of encroachment on land or property demands an intervention by the community or Jirga. The other option is armed conflict.

Monetary Disputes

Monetary transactions are usually done on verbal promises as tribal and rural Pukhtoons can not afford and do not desire to approach formal government courts to institute financial claims. The transactions are built on the fragile interpersonal relationship in which word of mouth promises more security than a written deed.

If a debtor fails to repay his debt, the creditor obtains the right of seizing the cattle or a person from the family of the debtor. The person kidnapped under Bramta is usually kept well and the community is informed of such an activity thus differentiating it from kidnapping for ransom.

Bota and Bramta in the tribal areas have often given rise to intertribal disputes and blood feuds. The British Government in India often resorted to Bramta in the event of hostilities with the tribesmen. When the Government failed to cow the tribesmen by force, it used to resort to this coercive method by seizing cattle, property, men, and women in Bramta. Even today, the tribal administration of the Government of Pakistan often resorts to the seizing of shops, vehicles, and men of a tribe accused under the law. Similarly, the tribal people use this tactic to put demands on the government by kidnapping government officials. When they need to recover their claims from private citizens of other areas, they can kidnap even a relative of the respondents under Bramta.

INDIVIDUALISM & COMMUNAL ASPECTS OF THE PUKHTOON SOCIETY

Individuals have rights, as well as society as a whole. How this is balanced in a Pukhtoon society is a complicated issue. While security of the individuals and families is a legitimate personal issue, all other factors of social life are subject to scrutiny by the community, usually lead by a Jirga. An individual detached from society is a non-entity[30], but to preserve one's own character, a man has the right to challenge the structures of the social order.

Within Pukhtoonwali, an individual finds enough liberties to assert himself in times of need. When honor is threatened, a Pukhtoon would not hesitate to take up arms, not as an allowance by the society, but as a right given to him by birth. However, the same society would control the liberties of the individual when it comes to conformation to the code of Pukhtoonwali. Popular belief is that the individual outside community has nothing to live for.

---

30   Meeras Khan, a remote rural interviewee from Kurram Agency

Community life to Pukhtoons is the only sure way to achieve security and progress. Practiced over centuries in the same manner, communal life has given balance to the various human needs of the individuals. Obviously, for such an arrangement, the context has to be very high. Therefore, individuals are perceived to be fully responsible for the conduct of their family members within the community. Under these conditions Jirga finds it easy to engage the family heads to sort out conduct of the youth. Putting a penalty on fathers or brothers instead of the actual culprit is a common feature of the Jirga decisions. On the other hand, it is true that an individual would rarely fail his or her community during such a Jirga trial by the community.

Pukhtoons live in close communities. The relationships among immediate family members in a household or home come first. To its people, a general appreciation of the relationship between parents and children comes from two main factors. First, the male children will ensure security to the family and will be the main source of bread earning. Second, the children will serve as pillars to their ageing parents.

Male children grow up with the mission to become a source of income for the collective household; to provide food, shelter, clothing, and medicine and to improve their standards of living. To earn a livelihood, they would go to other countries and for years live alone while their parents would look after the daughters-in-law and their grandchildren. Additionally, these growing children would want to do fresh constructions because of the growing size of the families and, secondly, they would want to purchase some lands. Side by side, these growing children prepare themselves to support the flow of Pukhtoonwali and to carry forward their inherited social order to the coming generations. Pukhtoonwali thus is repeated, trusted, and sustained by old and young a like.

SUMMARY[31]

The cultural and traditional phenomena vary from tribe to tribe and area to area, but the crux of the Pukhtoon society is based on the elements of Pukhtoonwali, the verbal code for Pukhtoons. This code is a doctrine, a law, rule, system and a way of life, which also facilitates

---

31 More can be found on Pukhtoon culture at the weblinks given in the bibliography

the meshing of modern practices and traditions to incorporate some sort of modernization and change.

In a broad sense, hospitality, magnanimity, chivalry, honesty, uprightness, patriotism, love and devotion are the essential features of Pukhtoonwali. Pukhtoon heritage and Pukhtoonwali is transmitted through oral traditions passed down from parents and elders to the coming generations.

Pukhtoon society practices a combination of norms and ethos unusual to others, but this combination gives shape to a perfectly developed way of living for a society. They have been living like this for ages now and they will make sure that they go on living like that, come what may! "Change? Yes we would accept it, but let's see what it means for us?" is a common motto for Pukhtoons.

Pukhtoon heritage and Pukhtoonwali is transmitted through an oral tradition passed down from parents to children in their homes and from elders to youngsters in Hujras. Pukhtoonwali is also considered a code of honor and its offshoots are hospitality, asylum and personal independence.

The Pukhtoon doctrine governs the life of individual Pukhtoons as well as their communities. Honor in Pukhtoonwali is the core for almost every issue. Second to that come issue of land and money.

One cannot judge the culture of Pukhtoons based on individual factors such as their love for history, or the role of women or other cultural traits like hospitality, asylum or enmity. It is neither our intention to make judgments, however, for understanding Jirga, one will need to understand the overall context in which Jirga operates. The interdependence of Jirga and the code of Pukhtoonwali or Pukhtoon culture provide us with enough reasons to treat the subject of Pukhtoon culture with as much weight as our study of the mainstream practice of Jirga, itself. Through studying this context, we wish to address some distinctive and yet outstanding issues that attract immediate judgment from outsiders and also look for opportunities to enable the Pukhtoon culture to find space to grow and keep pace with time.

CHAPTER 3

Exploring Jirga

TYPES OF JIRGA

Jirga is done at all levels of the society for different purposes and different objectives. For an outsider, the dynamics of Jirga may appear overwhelmingly complex, but upon deeper examination it is clear that a common understanding exists among Pukhtoons regarding these complexities.

The composition of a Jirga may be categorized in two ways. One is the representative level of a Jirga where the Jirga may represent a party, a village, or an area or region. In the second level, the Jirga serves a particular role, which can vary depending on the circumstances. Some examples of these roles are diplomatic missions, peacebuilding interventions, or small juries.

Locals use the term Jirga for many meanings. Some of these are:

Terms used for Jirga	Meaning
Jirga Kawal	Doing a Jirga or let's sit to talk
Pa Jirga talal	Going as a Jirga, or doing an intervention
Jirgay ta Khabara workawal	Referring a case to Jirga by parties or one of the parties
The Jirgay Khabara	The word of Jirga, opinion of Jirga
Jirga manz ta Ratlal	Intervention by a Jirga, i.e., ceasefire

Each of these terms is used for a variety of meanings related to the organization of the local community life, indicating the relevance and importance of Jirga as an integral institution to Pukhtoon culture.

The nature and scope of a specific Jirga can vary and there is generally no clear distinction between types of Jirga. Even the locals will talk about Jirga as the type they best understand, but when questioned, they smile and agree that their definition or understanding of a Jirga is a narrow one. Most writers have delineated Jirga into four general types: Sarkari, Qaumi/ Ulusi, Shakhsi, and Loya Jirga.

Sarkari or Governmental Jirga

Sarkari Jirga refers to a Jirga sponsored by the government. In the tribal areas of NWFP, the British established a contract with the locals allowing them to settle all issues between themselves and the government through a local Jirga. This contract was pronounced through the "Frontier Crimes Regulation of 1901 Act" allowing a representative of the government to regulate the formation and reformation of Jirga(s).

Under Frontier Crimes Regulation (FCR) 1901, the magistrate, the political agent or his assistant can designate a group of elders to try a criminal or civil case. The FCR authorizes settlement of quarrels by this Jirga. Jirga members, two or more depending on the nature and importance of the case, are nominated arbitrarily by the concerned government official. The Jirga calls the parties, analyzes the evidence, and recommends a verdict to be considered for approval by the government authority. There is an appellate tribunal of the government that then examines the Jirga decision. This Jirga can recommend a maximum penalty of up to fourteen years imprisonment and pass awards based on the local traditions. The political agent can approve such recommendation and enforce the decision.

The main components of the Sarkari Jirga are:

- A government representative
- A case registered by one of the parties or cognizance of a situation by the government
- Written referral of the case to the Jirga nominated by the government official
- Recording of statements of the parties by the Jirga
- Visits to the disputed sites by the Jirga members
- Recording of further evidence by the Jirga members
- Presentation of recommendations to the government agent
- Consideration, approval, or disapproval of the recommendations
- Reference back to the same Jirga for reconsideration in light of new facts
- Announcement of the award
- Right of parties to appeal
- Implementation of the award

In this case, nomination of the Jirga members is the most sensitive element because selection of such members who lack the confidence of the community can put the whole process of Jirga at risk. Jirga members are selected from a panel of Malaks or liaison people maintained by the government. To maintain transparency, the government officials may ask the parties to mutually agree to nominate the members themselves. In case of a disagreement, parties are asked to nominate an equal number of Jirga members to represent their respective sides, and the government has the right to nominate the referee among them. In all cases, however, the decision of the Jirga members is unanimous. In case of a dissent by one of the members, the same is noted on records similar to the proceedings of a jury.

Qaumi/ Ulusi or Local-Representative Jirga

Ulas means people and Qaum[32] means community. Thus, Ulasi Jirga is an assembly of the elders comprising each household of a certain village or community. It is convened to discuss matters such as collective property, rights and distribution of irrigation water, or common concerns, like the selection of a site for a school, etc. Ulasi Jirga is announced after initial consultations of a few elderly leaders of the community, and it is announced through a Naqqara or band beat. The venue and time of such an assembly is also given. It is an open assembly in which each person is allowed to speak and all opinions are given space. The decision may be taken in one or more sessions if the issue needs private deliberations by different stakeholders.

The jurisdiction of this type of Jirga is much wider than any other type of Jirga. The Qaumi Jirga can take up any issue of national or community interest. A Qaumi Jirga can:

- Hold as many sessions as needed
- Undertake any issue of interest or concern to the community
- Announce any interim decisions
- Make new laws or rules for the tribe, like grazing rights, water rights, etc.
- Call for other ideas
- Invite volunteers as a work force
- Raise taxes for community work

---

[32] In the larger sense Qaum also means a nation.

- Go as a delegation or
- Send delegations to parties or
- Send delegations to the neighboring tribes (in case of an intertribal issue)
- Raise an Army (Lashkar) to punish an outlaw
- Declare war and peace with a neighboring tribe.

Attended by all males and, in some cases witnessed by women, this kind of a Jirga is led by different cadres of representatives. These may include a combination of the following:

- Spinczirie or the white bearded, meaning the elderly wise people of the village
- Jirgamar(s) [33] or professional intermediaries popular for their lifelong roles and experiences as peacebuilders
- Mahsar/Masharan or Leader/Leaders, usually a person of independent means, known for his leadership in the community
- Khan, or the noble, generally a landlord aristocrat known for his hospitality and magnanimity
- Religious leader or Clergy—much used as a consultant on family laws

In this kind of an assembly, all participants have a right to speak, but most prefer to observe only. Without any formal facilitator each one offers the other the opportunity to start the talk. In the end, someone begins with a tale or a narrative, setting the stage for a discussion on the issue. Various parameters of the issue are discussed by addressing the concerns of each individual from the community, while the leadership listens and facilitates further talk. Finally, a common ground is identified and announced for agreement by all.

Shakhsi or Third-Party Jirga

This Jirga is formulated in the case of a dispute that arises between two individuals or families. The Jirga members are chosen from both of the parties or both parties agree to the nomination of neutral members. Balance and neutrality are important in order for the members to arrive at a just settlement that is acceptable to both sides. Failure of one party or the other to accept the verdict of the Jirga puts the credibility of the .

---

[33] Professional Intermediaries

Jirga at stake, creating a situation where the original Jirga becomes a party in a second or even third Jirga. Until both parties voluntarily agree to accept such a verdict, or until the Jirga has the powers and resources to mobilize a Badraga[34] for implementation of their decision, a misjudgment by the Jirga will not stand the test of Justice. Again raising the Badraga brings the Jirga's decision to the awareness of the whole community, thus keeping the process in check. Because the process of Shakhsi Jirga involves adjudication of the dispute through a process similar to arbitration, credibility is crucial.

The following steps are involved in Shakhsi Jirga:

- One of the parties approaches certain members of the community known as "Jirgamar," states an issue and asks for intervention, or
- Both the parties agree to settle their dispute through third party intervention.
- The Jirgamar approached by the parties gives an initial hearing and advises the party or the parties on an appropriate direction.
- The Jirgamars may advise the party or parties to involve other people more appropriate for the case.
- Jirga members establish a channel of communication with and between the parties.
- On minor issues, the Jirga establishes a face saving norm to settle the matter publicly
- If the issue is complex and involves due judgment by the Jirga, parties are asked to delegate powers to the Jirga to decide the issue (This is also known as "Waak" or consent of the parties).
- Parties give unconditional powers to the interveners to decide the issue between them.
- Parties are asked to deposit surety or bond[35], which can be confiscated later if one of the parties decides to withdraw from the consent given earlier.
- Jirga hears the parties, sometimes face to face, at other times one after the other.

---

[34] A security force of volunteers, raised to secure and protect the proceedings of a specific Jirga.

[35] Usually weapons or cattle or cash money is taken from the party, depending on the nature of the dispute.

- The situation is placed openly before both the parties at all stages of negotiation, or
- The parties are told only the good side of the story, while the Jirgamars search for common ground.
- After clarifying the issues with both the parties, taking all possible evidence and applying the local traditional laws, Jirga gives a verdict, which both parties must accept.
- In case a party does not publicly accept such a verdict on grounds of injustice, the same party must convince a more credible Jirga to intervene and reconsider the issue.
- When the Jirga members and the community are convinced of malice by one party, such a party is socially cornered and the victim gets the legitimacy to engage in self-defense.
- In such a situation, the Jirga might even call for raising a militia (Badraga) from the community to enforce such a decision.

Loya or Grand Jirga

Loya Jirga, or the grand assembly, is a process through which representatives of various areas organize to discuss and vote on issues at the national level. A question about the representative status of these participants is usually quite sensitive and, if the Jirga is even slightly mishandled, the credibility of this national level process quickly looses its efficacy. As discussed earlier, representation or selection of members of the Jirga is a delicate process. Each representative must have the unquestionable confidence of the community he represents and each community must be duly represented at such a Jirga. Each member must be heard at the conference and concerns raised by a member must be taken into account while collective decisions are being made. All decisions of a Jirga must be unanimous.

The institution of Loya Jirga in Afghanistan has gained legitimacy as a constitution-making body because of the frequency of its practice. There is no fixed size for this kind of a Jirga. The framework for representation is defined by the convening authority, where each administrative unit is allowed to bring forward a representative. Major tribes are also given rights to send representatives and similarly special representation may be allowed for women and minorities. This is a one off assembly convened to address a specific issue or situation of highest national interest.

The process of selection of the representatives is often tedious, as there must be a universal agreement to the framework through which the nominations are made. Different methods of selection are applied by the central government, but rarely has the government been able to find an undisputed formula to represent the whole width and breadth of its population. As such, each geographical district and each major and minor tribe must be judiciously represented.

Outside Afghanistan, the concept of Loya Jirga is applied at the geographical agency[36] level in the Federally Administered Tribal Areas (FATA) as well. The Loya Jirga of a particular agency might be formed to discuss an issue with an adjoining agency. Subsequently a Loya Jirga of all the tribal districts (agencies) may be formed to raise an issue collectively with the government or to set up a new law for the collective tribal life.

The selection of the members of a Loya Jirga is also done through the process of Jirga. Small and mid-level Jirgas representing communities choose their representatives for a higher level Jirga.

SELECTION OF THE JIRGA

Process of selection of Jirga is quite delicate as credibility of the entire process of Jirga depends on the nature of selection of Jirga members. This "selection of the Jirga members varies according to the type of Jirga"[37]. Under the FCR 1901, the Political Agent or his assistant is empowered to nominate members who comprise a Jirga. These members of Sarkari Jirga are usually selected from the notable elders or the Malaks of the area who are registered as people loyal to the government. In a Shakhsi Jirga, parties select or approve selection of members of Jirga who may be totally neutral towards the parties or the parties may nominate their respective members to represent their interests. In this case, the parties also mutually agree to nominate an odd number of neutral members such that the Jirga is expected to reach a judicious decision in the light of the code of Pukhtoonwali. In the case of the Ulusi Jirga, the members are usually comprised of elders

---

[36] Agency is a tribal administrative district

[37] www.khyber.org/pashtoculture/Jirga/Jirgas.shtml (Dr. Mumtaz Bangash)

of the notable families whose social standing and experience with the Pukhtoonwali entitles them to a place on the council. This is a more popular process of nomination in which status of Jirga members is representative of the people they speak for. There is no limit on the size of the Jirga as it varies from situation to situation, "based on the nature, significance and sensitivity of the dispute. It might consist of one member, although two members are more usual and often there are four or six experienced members, fully conversant with the laws of the Pukhtoonwali"[38].

We have observed that selection of the Jirga can happen in four ways: by the parties, due to personal aptitude, by the community, and by the government. The next four sections expand on dimensions of each selection process.

Selection by the Parties

In a particular case, one of the parties can approach a person of repute to help the situation from worsening. This could be a plea, a complaint, a warning, or all of the above. At this point, one or both parties feel that if intervention does not occur soon, things may get complicated for either of the parties and for the community as well. The person so approached is bound to analyze the issue and strategize to present the case before an appropriate group of people. Such a group may be comprised of the immediate relatives, friends, neighbors, Khan, religious leadership or professional Jirgamars (peace builders). Depending on what is best for the situation, the matter may be taken up with the appropriate number and cadre of people who should consider this party's plea. At that point a case is instituted before a Jirga. It should be noted that in Pukhtoon society, each male member is almost equally qualified for his role as an intervener, as there are hardly any hierarchies among the men in this system.

The case may be moved from level to level in the Pukhtoon social structure, i.e., from less professional to more professional members of society. Depending upon who can effectively handle the situation, an appropriate tier takes the cognizance, and an approach to the opposite party is appropriately made to obtain a defense plea or plea in reply. This approach to the other party is a very calculated move. Carefully

---

38 www.khyber.org/pashtoculture/Jirga/Jirgas.shtml (Dr. Mumtaz Bangash)

selected words are used so that the party is not offended at the outset. As mentioned earlier, refusal to entertain a Jirga is a disgraceful act by a party and puts the party in a situation of social isolation, which few people can afford, particularly when confronted with a conflict situation.

Personal Aptitude

Unlike in the case of interpersonal disputes, the community accepts a few men known for their passion, interest, and skills to practice professional peacebuilding through Jirga. With an aptitude for professional peacebuilding, these Jirgamars are highly proactive masters of strategizing, fluent in the use of proverbs and idioms, and fully committed to the cause of peacebuilding.

Such freelance professionals win the confidence of their respective communities, as well as the neighboring people, obtaining the status of trusted representatives of the people. Without any formal elections, they are often called by the government or outside agencies to represent the society and negotiate on their behalf. Although allowed to make decisions independently, they rarely fail the communities at various forums, thus assuring the continued support of the community. Although they have the confidence of the community, Jirgamars may not make critical decisions regarding the stake of the communities they represent unless they obtain the approval of the community.

Selection by the Community

The community allows a few professionals or other "white bearded" to form a Jirga when an issue arises. The nature of issue may relate to an individual (including a female in this case), a family or the whole community. Such stakeholders approach the known elders for intervention. These Jirga members thus become representatives of the stakeholders and are accountable to them as well as the community (for their role) in a true democratic spirit. The composition and size then depends on the nature of the issue and the stakes of the community.

Selection by Khan or the Government

The government official or an influential person of the area may also nominate people to address a specific question. A call for Jirga by the government or by a Khan is not a classical form of Jirga. However, when the stakes are high this process is keenly attended by the genuine community representatives who form the Jirga. This kind of a Jirga does not enjoy the level of credibility with the parties that the indigenous Jirga has. Despite this drawback, such a Jirga can play a vital role in supporting the parties to reach an amicable settlement of their dispute, based on the level of sincerity of the Government or Khan and the character of the Jirgamars

CRITERIA FOR SELECTION

Community members observe the qualities of individual men, starting from their youth, to see who may emerge as a promising professional. These people generally have the following characteristics:

- Visible attendance in social events
- Regular presence in Hujra
- Regular attendance in the company of elders in Hujra
- A good knowledge of history
- A good knowledge of Pukhtoonwali
- Little "loose" talk used ever in life
- Proactive intervention in situations demanding attention
- Good sense of humility, sympathy, respect, and understanding
- Particular attendance to offer condolences
- Reaching out to farther villages at marriage and birth ceremonies
- Maintaining contact with the community
- Maintaining an upright character
- Belonging to reasonably better off and better known families
- Making correct choices when taking sides with victims at different times in their lives
- Sacrificing their time, energy, and money for the sake of peacebuilding
- A spotless history of honesty, integrity and uprightness

SUMMARY

Without any specific knowledge as to its place and time of origin, Jirga remains an effective institution for peaceful communications and resolution of disputes among individuals, communities, and tribes.

The system of Jirga is passed down from generation to generation without any written protocols or written form of terms and conditions. It is considered a vital customary judicial institution where all people are considered equal before the process. In most cases, conflicts are resolved in an acceptable manner and everybody respects the results of the Jirga. However, stronger enforcement may also be needed to bring justice.

Jirga offers a medium of communication between rival groups and tribes, as well as mediators, but beyond that Jirga is a means for creating a structure and venue to address differences between groups in conflict. In addition, the Jirga may be thought of as a jury because of its nature of composition and involvement. The Jirga system ensures effective participation of the people in administering justice and makes sure that justice is manifestly done. Jirga also gives protection and security to the weaker party in a conflict.

CHAPTER 4

Dynamics of Jirga

FUNCTIONS OF COMMUNITY LEVEL JIRGAS

There are three main functions of Jirga at the community level: dispute resolution, community-wide issue-driven Jirga, and inter-family Jirga. The following three sections examine each in detail.

Dispute Resolution

In this Jirga, the parties, as major stakeholders, have a considerable amount of influence. There are three approaches that can begin the dispute resolution process within the Jirga.

I. One of the parties approaches the Jirga members:
In this case, members who are requested to intervene, act as
a.   Fact finders,
b.   Advocates,
c.   Facilitators,
d.   Mediators, or
e.   Jury

The Jirga member's initial response would be to find out more about the situation and to clarify the issues. This typically involves spreading the word into the community that a disputant has requested an intervention. More is discovered about the history of the dispute and its various dynamics through talks with women at the disputant's home and male friends at Hujra.

The second party in the dispute, which already finds the news of the initiative of the first party, is usually ready to receive the Jirga. This way a dialogue would start to clarifying issues, finding alternatives and approaching a resolution acceptable to both the parties.

If the second party shows arrogance and does not respond well to the queries by the interveners, blame is placed on the second party for being non-cooperative. This gives the first party a moral edge over the other.

When there is compliance, the interveners facilitate the process of clarifying issues and settling the dispute. Agreement to the final decision by the parties is crucial.

Parties may be advised by the Jirga members to go for arbitration, if it is difficult for the parties to reach an agreement. Again, rules of arbitration are applied and selection of arbitrators is done with the consent of the parties.

II.   Jirga approaches the disputants:

Conflict escalates relatively quickly when there may be a history of violence between the parties or the parties may be emotionally charged. In this case, a Jirga is formed to prevent the situation from getting worse. The Jirga must be announced and an agreement of procedure must be cleared by the elders and influential members of the community. After approval is gained, the interveners have the go ahead to establish an intervention and parties are advised to hold their fire. One of the parties will hold fire first, while the interveners approach the second party. A temporary ceasefire is thus established, leveling the ground for further talks. Rules of mediation or arbitration are thereafter applied to the case.

III.   Both parties decide to approach the Jirga:

A situation where both the parties desire the help of interveners is relatively easier to organize. Steps involved in mediation and arbitration are thus followed.

Community-wide Issue-driven Jirga

A Jirga is formed when an issue of importance arises in the community. The issue is generally related to the collective living of the community, such as development or security, and any action taken must reflect the collective view of the community. The issue is discussed informally at first by the elders in the Hujra, a sitting place for the community elders where evening chat takes place to review various aspects of life in the community. As this smaller group of elders discusses the issue, they can decide that the issue requires the attention of the larger community. The same issue is taken from one Hujra to another and views are exchanged between the elders of the community. If need be, a collective body can be formed with the consent of all the influential men and having uniform representation from all the stakeholders. A grand assembly is announced for public debate on the issue, which is attended by members of the community. Jirga members facilitate the talk, while playing with small stones laid before them on the ground, or mapping the argument by drawing figures on the ground with a small stick. Such an assembly may make a decision on the issue or may postpone it for another session or an upcoming event.

Inter-family Jirga

Closely related to the first category, the third function of the Jirga is really a delegation of one family, clan, or group that proposes a new idea to another family, clan, or group. This is generally a dispute-free issue and more a proposal of a social or development nature. For example, a family can decide to send a delegation to another family for making a match for their children. Alternatively, a delegation can be sent for proposing sale or purchase of land to another party. Sending a message through a third party is a safe way to set a stage for advancing the talk.

WHO IS A JIRGAMAR (INTERVENER)?

The make up of a Jirga is very important to the outcome of the case. If the wrong kind of person is allowed to lead a Jirga, the outcome may dwindle in uncertainties. Who, then, can be a Jirgamar, or intervener? Jirgamars are of two types. There are the professional people, holding the title of Malak and devoting their lives to live as self-appointed leaders of the community. The second type consists of people of independent means who have influence in the community. These influential community members do not do third party intervention in all cases, but can articulate a situation and can argue a case well before another party.

There are different aspects of the personality of a Jirgamar or intervener in the Pukhtoon communities. The Jirgamar should be well versed with the code of Pukhtoonwali. The education of Pukhtoonwali comes through a lifelong association with peers, regular attendance in Hujra, a long career of representation as a junior member of delegations, and maintaining a neat and clean character record throughout life. In most cases, Jirgamars will not indulge in personal enmities or disputes, and if they do, they would have their things resolved gracefully and quickly.

A second aspect of the personality of a Jirgamar is his understanding of and loyalty to the code of Pukhtoonwali. Pukhtoonwali, in addition to other things, dictates it followers a strict code of honesty, dignity, strong character and pursuit of justice for all. Therefore some people with better understanding of Pukhtoonwali but lesser intervention skills may prove to be more effective Jirgamars than ones who may have spent their lives in the process, turned white bearded, but may grown little as Pukhtoons and professional Jirgamars.

A third aspect is the capability of a person to articulate a situation well, use the right rhetoric, idioms, and stories, as well as references to the past. Idioms and phrases play a decisive role in the process of Jirga, as the use of the right idiom at the right time by one of the wise Jirga members can resolve an intractable conflict for the disputants. The use of idioms and proverbs also makes it easy for the local communities to understand complex issues in a simple manner.

Fourthly, Jirgamars are skilled at conflict analysis. Within the context of Pukhtoonwali and drawing on their strong belief in peace, the people of Jirga have aptitudes to analyze a particular situation technically, draw deductions, forecast the future, and take strategic actions to prevent bloodshed and enmities in their communities. These aptitudes are not formally taught to them but they come with the experience of peacebuilding and learning from their peers in the profession. For a Jirga member, the understanding of the outcome of a specific conflict comes as a sixth sense, a peculiar intuition that serves as a stimulus to act in the right direction.

Conflict analysis is done as a practical process of analyzing and understanding the reality of the conflict from a variety of perspectives, which forms the basis of selecting the most effective strategies for a particular conflict. This is done with a number of simple, practical, and generic tools and techniques giving the Jirga a better understanding of the situation and helping them choose appropriate tools for intervention.

One ingrained technique that Jirga members use is to pay special attention to the narratives that parties use during the conflict. The narratives explain their position and assumptions regarding the issues and help the Jirga understand the context of the conflict.

Members of Jirga are very skilled at conflict analysis. Knowledge of the history of a conflict works as a first step towards understanding the conflict and its nature. As locals, Jirga members have a surprising memory of the important local events and incidents. Elderly people add to the knowledge base of youngsters about the history of families and their disputes. An overview of the timelines, equated with the "kill score" of each party, determines the psychological status of the parties. The psychological status is further studied in light of the material losses and potential gains for each party, if the conflict persists. Within the context of Pukhtoonwali, worldviews of parties are assessed and a cost benefit analysis for each party is done to build an argument for peace. Factors such as trauma healing, and sensitivities like identity, dignity, and ego issues are well considered before launching a strategic intervention.

Finally, the peacebuilding characteristics of Jirga are frequently associated with religion. Jirgamars draw on the teachings of Islam on peace and peacebuilding as well as their own cultural background that legitimizes their professional and social roles.

In summary, Jirgamars are driven by their passion for social leadership. In the absence of a system that relies on a formal election process, these people have no choice but to offer their services voluntarily to the community. The community can scrutinize all such contestants for their character, capacity and past conduct. Having passed the test, these Jirgamars need to retain the confidence of the society to remain in the loop. Jirgamars move up the Jirga hierarchy by maintaining a selfless and people-friendly attitude throughout their lives. These people grow up to command respect from the community and be called Masharan, or social leaders.

Ready for an all out war and relying on a strong rhetoric of peace, Jirgamars are pacifists of their own kind. Relying heavily on the language of peace and peacebuilding, they frequently use references of religion to convince parties to give up arms. In addition to active pleading for peace and gaining the confidence of the parties, withdrawal, avoidance, patience and tolerance are their major tools to achieve peace. A pro-active intervention is a passion for which Jirga people risk even their own lives and spend their own money and time in order to live a life of professional satisfaction.

ESSENTIALS OF JIRGA

The Context

Jirga can be formed at an interpersonal level, at the village or community level, and even at national levels. One primary aspect of the Jirga, however, is the framework or the context in which Jirga is formed. This context is the code of Pukhtoonwali. One cannot understand the dynamics of Jirga without understanding the forces that keep the institution alive. Pukhtoonwali forms the field in which Jirga can be applied.

The Jirga works best within the context of Pukhtoonwali as Pukhtoonwali provides the set of rules, regulations, laws, ethos, and moral standards, justifying the theoretical framework of Pukhtoonwali—a context for an indigenous, independent, traditional, collective, and communal group of people. It is the common culture, in which the meanings of issues related to social justice are located and identified.

The Parties

A dispute resolution Jirga must function with the parties who conform to the same code of Pukhtoonwali. When the parties belong to different contexts, the Jirga must become a body to undertake negotiations or mediation, but not arbitration.

Geographical Contiguity

Jirga changes its role and approaches towards the parties depending on the geographical location of the parties. Three scenarios can be identified for the changing roles of Jirga. Firstly, when the parties reside in close proximity and belong to the same tribe or community. In this case the Jirga cannot ignore a situation calling for third party intervention or public peace will be in danger. The Jirga in such a case undertakes intervention and usually end as playing the role of arbitrators. Secondly, when the parties are distant apart, the Jirga of one village will require approaching the elders of the other village where the second party resides. This way, group of the two elders will decide what course can be taken to resolve the issue between such disputants. Elders of the two villages in such a case will first deliberate on the issue themselves and then in consultation with the parties may agree to form a collective Jirga, or ask one of the Jirgas to look after the issue. Thirdly, when the parties reside in different areas and do not share the same code of Pukhtoonwali, the Jirga of a complainant will approach the other party as a delegate or council of the complainant party. This is more of a diplomatic role in which they represent the interests of the party on whose initiative this Jirga was sent.

PRINCIPLES OF JIRGA

Few broad principles explained below are key to a successful Jirga.

Transparency

The word "Jirga" is said to be comprised of "Jar," meaning to say things openly, while "ga" is a suffix, which is said to mean, "place." Mostly held in the open air, the element of transparency is a hallmark of the process of Jirga. The matter is discussed and argued in public in the presence of the community. When people are clear about the proceedings of the Jirga, they duly support the efforts and the Jirga moves along with the opinion of the community as a whole. Hence, the Jirga needs to maintain a completely transparent relationship with the community, educating people about the facts, exploring options on a subject, deducing logical conclusions, and offering an undisputed opinion for the community. This transparent method creates the support base for the decisions of the Jirga.

Confidence of the Community

Having the confidence of the people is a principle that establishes the connection between transparency and accountability. When the Jirga members do not carry the confidence of the people, their opinions carry little value, and decisions made by them cannot be implemented. When there are popular perceptions of mischief or partisanship in a Jirga, the community can get together to raise a more popular based Jirga to confront the injustice supported by the malicious Jirga.

Unanimity

Another striking aspect of the process of Jirga is that after a thorough debate and discussion on a specific issue, the decision regarding the process or the outcome is made unanimously. Only in exceptional cases it is observed that the Jirga, like a jury, can give a split decision regarding the outcome. There must be unanimity in the process, however.

Since implementation of a decision is the most important element of the process of dispute resolution, Jirga decisions have to be practicable or agreeable to both the parties. The Jirga would raise Arbaki, its security force, only in exceptional cases. Therefore all decisions of the Jirga must have built-in mechanisms to ensure implementation. While social pressure plays a role in obliging the parties to conform to the decisions of the Jirga, the decision must look reasonable to the parties as well. The parties may be required to adjust their interests slightly left or right, but they must mutually agree to the decision of the Jirga. In this sense, all decisions of the Jirga should represent a possible agreement by the parties. In some cases, this agreement is sought from the parties while exploring ideas and brainstorming separately with the parties.

One way of seeking this mutual agreement as practiced by the Jirgas is to obtain the consent of the parties, called a Waak, before the start of the proceedings. This unconditional consent, written or verbally given, turns the process of the Jirga from mediative intervention to a judicial arbitration. In the legal sense, arbitration involves a procedure for implementation of the decision of arbitrators, which in the case of settled areas means an arbitration award turning into a court decree to be implemented by police. In the tribal setup, although Jirga members can call for raising a volunteer force to enforce a decision, but it is not mandatory in all cases. This discretion gives enormous powers to Jirga over the parties who are real stakeholders in the process. Giving a Waak or surrendering one's rights therefore, on the one hand, may result in a just decision by the Jirga, which will require forced implementation. In the absence of a standard rule for implementation procedure, some quality decisions may remain unimplemented. On the other hand, there may come to light some low quality decisions which might be unduly implemented through force, thus damaging the credibility of the Jirga.

In many cases, parties are asked to deposit sureties or bonds like weapons or cash money as prior agreement to the eventual decision of the Jirga. This is a useful practice for longstanding and intractable disputes, in which the Jirga wants the parties to move forward and forget about the age-old bitterness. High cost sureties in such cases help the Jirgas make tough decisions that will allow the parties to overcome their chosen traumas of the past.

Freedom of Speech

Each Jirga member and all the people witnessing the Jirga proceedings have absolute freedom to speak. There are two aspects to this freedom. One is that anyone can raise an issue regarding the process or composition of a Jirga and announce a disagreement. The second aspect is that there is the space for anyone to comment on the content. As per the tradition, people are allowed to carry personal arms like guns and rifles to the venue of the Jirga. Only rarely does a Jirga setting become a physical battleground between the parties represented. The security of the place is assured by the decorum and discipline of the proceedings, the presence of the elders, and the leadership's control of the gathering.

Accountability Process of Jirga Members

Working as an informal team of co-professionals, Jirga members recognize and appreciate efforts of everyone working towards peace and peacebuilding. However, the elders are always alert to the presence of miscreant in their professional community. The society exercises a system of internal control over the people who aspire for leadership in an informal way. As soon as someone is suspected of misusing the process of Jirga or abusing his powers as a Jirga member, the elders must decide to expose such person and publicly dissociate themselves from him, a punishment with which few can afford to live.

Accusations about the use of bribes and bias or partiality by one or more Jirga members can be heard frequently in the tribal areas where the Government of Pakistan acts as a stakeholder in the process. The community, however, as an informal local institution, has little tolerance for this kind of an attitude. Members of the Jirga accused of partiality or accepting bribes are immediately exposed before the community, putting a permanent dent on their character and their ability to lead the community any further.

Message of Peace

In the middle of a violent conflict, the best tool to counter the vengeful side of Pukhtoonwali is to preach the philosophy of peace. A Jirga can emphasize religion, the danger of loss of life or property, and the importance of children and their education to convince warring parties to refrain from violence. Jirga's overwhelming reliance and belief on the ideology of pacifism gives them a remarkable edge during a potentially violent situation.

In striking contrast to the message of peace, Jirga, like the Pukhtoon society in general, justifies an all out war as a last resort. Life to Pukhtoons is a trust of God to be spent with dignity and honor, as defined by the society over time. However, a message of peace always remains an attractive tool with the Jirga to initiate a strong dialogue during a conflict situation.

CHAPTER 5

Processes of Jirga

There are many different perceptions of what Jirga is and what it is not. To some, Jirga is sacred and holy. For others it is a dispute resolution body, and for even others it is the "guardian angel" of society. To add complexity, Jirga is used with many suffixes and prefixes to apply a common understanding to the varic.s forms and roles of Jirga. Since the definition of Jirga is based on local understandings and dependant upon the social leadership, Jirga can be hijacked by influential and monopolizers with the intention of accruing undue benefits and exploiting the weak. Given these varied perceptions, definitions, nd uses, it is important that each pattern of Jirga be given a distinct name so that the common understanding becomes shared and legitimate. Space is then created for Jirga to operate in more complex and challenging situations. Based on our research and comparisons with more universally known terms for conflict resolution, we have attempted to define and categorize the distinctive forms of Jirga. The basic forms fall under the categories of facilitation, mediation, arbitration, and advocacy.

FACILITATION

Facilitation is a process by which a third party helps to coordinate the activities of a person or a group, acts as a process facilitator during meetings, or helps a group prevent or manage tension and move productively toward decisions. Facilitation is "a collaborative process used to help parties discuss issues, identify and achieve goals and complete tasks in a mutually-satisfactory manner. This process uses an impartial third party, the facilitator, who focuses on the processes and procedures of dispute resolution and decision-making. The facilitato. is impartial to the issues being discussed, rarely contributes substantive ideas and has no decision-making authority"[39].

Within the Pukhtoon cultural framework, there are two places that serve as informal forums for community facilitation. One is Hujra, a

---

[39] http://www.saskjustice.gov.sk.ca/DisputeResolution/glossary.shtml

community owned place for the male members to get together in the evenings and discuss community issues or pass time. The second is the street mosque where people with religious orientation find space to discuss issues in the light of Islam and seek the opinion of the Imam (pastor).

In the traditional Jirga, however, the rules of facilitation differ from the ones in Hujra or the Mosque. In the Jirga process, the Jirga members would go to the Hujra or house of the concerned party and discuss the issue. The same Jirga might do a separate facilitation for the other party in that party's house. The value attached to going to someone's place in Pukhtoonwali is synonymous with the concept of becoming a guest. Since a guest is assured safety, respect, and space, the party concerned cannot afford to be rude to the visitors. This is a form of separate facilitation in which the ground is leveled for a one to one talk between the parties. In this pre-mediation stage, the interveners or the Jirga members sort out many issues between the parties by removing confusions and identifying common ground between the parties. This kind of initial facilitation may even be undertaken secretly as sometimes the intervener may feel that the process of mediation will be hindered by some other stakeholders in malicious ways. This is true particularly when the elders of a party or group might want to resolve the issue, but the youngsters are eager to take revenge in the light of Pukhtoonwali. The elders therefore can use their prerogative to advance the talk before the youth can escalate the conflict. A decision of elders as such is binding upon the youngsters of the concerned party.

In another form of facilitated intervention, community leaders invite the public to come forward to discuss issues of importance for the community and make collective decisions. The art of collective facilitation is practiced within the context of Pukhtoonwali where elders allow freedom of speech to the youngsters and junior members of the Jirga are encouraged to speak first. The leadership at the end summarizes the brainstorming and a collective decision is announced for approval of the community.

MEDIATION

"A structured dispute resolution process where an impartial third party, the mediator, meets with disputants in an effort to identify the issues, explore options and clarify goals. The mediator facilitates face-to-face meetings of the parties to assist them in reaching a mutually-acceptable agreement. Parties reach agreement freely, voluntarily and on the basis of informed consent. Mediation is assisted negotiation. As the "process expert," the mediator helps the parties negotiate efficiently and effectively"[40]. Mediation is a tool that provides third party intervention where parties undertake a structured and peaceful dialogue to decide their future course for themselves. The underlying assumption in this case is that the parties are empowered to take responsibility for their own lives and comfort. Mediation uses trained neutral third parties to help the parties in dispute "talk" their way to an agreeable solution. A mediator guides the "talk," ensuring that each person has the chance to present her or his views and suggestions for resolution. The disputing parties decide what issues need to be addressed and what resolutions best meet their needs. In Pukhtoon society, Pukhtoonwali provides the basic framework in which the mediation is undertaken.

Mediation is applied at all the stages of a conflict in Pukhtoon society. In the preventive role, interveners approach the parties when there are tensions between the parties and no clear violence has taken place. Interveners at this stage listen to the respective stories of the parties and help them come out with issues in a peaceful manner, so that possible solutions can be identified. This also helps the parties communicate their issues without meeting each other. If a positive level of communication is established at this stage, a violent stage of the conflict is avoided. The Jirga may hold separate sessions with the parties in the start, but eventually the purpose is to enable the parties to sit face to face and discuss the issue in a peaceful manner. In mediation, the interveners may not make recommendations to the parties, give their own advice or opinion, or predict what could happen if the conflict is allowed to escalate. This is done for two reasons. One is that the parties know what they are likely to face in case the conflict escalates, and secondly, identification of a future scenario, when the conflict is allowed to escalate towards violence, could highlight weaknesses of one party over the other. The weaker party may take this as an attack on their honor and get ready to respond with full fury, thus killing the purpose of a peacebuilding intervention.

---

[40] http://www.saskjustice.gov.sk.ca/DisputeResolution/glossary.shtml

When the Interveners find out that the parties are preparing to launch offensives against each other, the Jirga has little option but to plead or to insist that the parties remain peaceful so that a new Jirga, mutually agreed to by all parties, is formed to help them settle their issues. If violence does occur, the Jirga members once again go in as interveners to undertake mediation, such that parties are enabled to talk to each other through peaceful means. In some cases, the Jirga shuttles between the parties even when there is no immediate threat to peace or public tranquility. Jirga members may mediate between neighbors or close relatives who are not on talking terms with each other.

Jirga members are neutral in the process. Their neutrality towards issues earns them the confidence of the parties. To retain this confidence, Jirga refrains from taking sides or passing judgments or a decision. Sometimes this notion of neutrality is seriously challenged by those who think interveners must be biased towards the ultimate goal of achieving justice for the oppressed. When the Jirga members feel that a party is using coercion, or one party is too weak (physically, intellectually, socially or economically) to reasonably resist pressure from the other side, or one party is being too harsh, the Jirga, as peacebuilders, choose to take the side of the weak and oppressed in a suitable way.

Jirga applies reflective methods of storytelling and retelling with a focus on repairing the relationship. This is quite similar to the concept of transformative mediation in the western context. Transformative mediation focuses on restoration of the relationship in addition to resolution of issues. The important component of this kind of mediation is that the parties understand the human aspect of the dispute and recognize the needs and interests of the other party. This is undertaken exclusively as one method or combined with other methods of intervention.

Mediation defines a process, which enables the parties in the dispute to decide what is good for them. Keeping in mind the spirit of the ends of justice, mediators facilitate the process further by helping the parties identify issues, start from the common ground, and generate alternatives. It is necessary that the parties feel empowered in the process.

ARBITRATION

"The process by which the parties to a dispute submit their differences to the judgment of an impartial person or group appointed by mutual consent or statutory provision"[41] is called as arbitration. Unlike facilitation or mediation, arbitration involves making judgments, which implies that there needs to be a mechanism for implementation of these judgments. Therefore arbitration is generally viewed only in the context where formal legal framework is available. However, the concept of Arbitration has been in practice in all traditional societies for ages. As a society, Pukhtoons are inclined to offer, as well as undertake, arbitration more often than other methods of dispute resolution. This is particularly common in the tribal areas of NWFP and Balochistan where the interveners obtain the consent of the parties to decide about their issues, whether civil or criminal, through a Jirga. A similar pattern was also adopted in the Panchayat system in the Punjab province of Pakistan. Arbitration is most successful in corporate environments or on other civil disputes such as rent cases, labor, construction, and securities regulations, where an umbrella legal structure is available to support the processes of arbitration and enforce its outcome.

The process of arbitration offers a few benefits when compared with regular judicial litigation. It saves the time of the parties in comparison to the time it takes to have a civil case processed through a court of law. It also saves the time of the court, thus reducing the workload on the judiciary. The process is cheaper as it does not involve the expenses of hiring a lawyer and of paying court fees.

Arbitration can be seen as a simplified version of a judicial trial, involving simplified rules of evidence and few formalities. Both sides either agree on one arbitrator, or each side selects one arbitrator and the two arbitrators elect a third to comprise a panel. Arbitrators hear the parties, identify issues, collect necessary evidence and give a balanced verdict, which is not in contrast to the wider principles of justice and fair play. The decision of the arbitration cannot be appealed, however, subject to certain conditions, parties may ask for a review or revision of the decision.

---

[41] http://education.yahoo.com/reference/dictionary/

Neutral and independent individuals or groups like Jirga can work as arbitrators. In the tribal areas of Pakistan, FCR 1901 provides procedural rules that govern the arbitration process and a code of ethical conduct that governs the arbitrators' actions.

In the Pukhtoon culture, mediation is considered a weak intervention as the interveners or Jirga do not have enough powers to summon the parties, record the evidence, and announce decisions based on justice. The perception that mediation cannot provide resolution of disputes, particularly when the parties do not have personal capacities to handle the issues peacefully is quite valid. However, it is evident that many of the processes undertaken by the Jirga are more like the processes of mediation rather than arbitration.

In the government influenced tribal areas of Pakistan, the rules applied for Jirga as a body for arbitration are quite similar to the provisions of the "Arbitration Act of 1940" as enforced in Pakistan. The arbitrator could be mutually selected by the parties or the government official supervising the process may help the parties nominate an appropriate arbitrator. In some cases, the parties may be under a written contract or agreement to resolve their future disputes through a Jirga (arbitration). In other cases, the parties may agree to have their issues decided through arbitration rather than direct negotiation. The names of the arbitrators may be agreed upon by the parties at the time of writing a contract or a later date. All parties to a dispute must agree and trust the nomination of such arbitrators before the arbitration takes place, however. When the parties are unable to agree on the nomination of Jirga members, and still public peace is threatened, the community can form a Jirga to help resolve the issue. The Jirga may be supported by a force of volunteers or government forces to uphold a temporary truce until a mechanism for resolution is decided upon amicably.

ADVOCACY

Advocacy is "the act of pleading or arguing in favor of something, such as a cause, idea, or policy; active support"[42]. Primarily, Jirga as an institution advocates for the code of Pukhtoonwali. Within the code, Jirga tries to find and apply the basic principles of peace and justice

---

[42] http://education.yahoo.com/reference/dictionary/

such that ends of justice are achieved and every possible effort is made to undo the harm done to the victim.

Jirga can take the side of a weak party against a strong party by declaring that the high-headed party is a little too arrogant. Such blame by the Jirga is considered a serious violation of the norms of Pukhtoonwali that only few can afford.

A Jirga can also take up an issue of the collective cause and take action on the subject. In some cases in the settled districts of NWFP, Jirgas were able to put wildlife protection laws in place. Similarly, in the tribal areas of NWFP, many cases of promoting girls' education have been launched with the help of local Jirgas.

Similarly, in the Afghan refugee camps, NGOs and donors working on "mother and child health programs" needed access to women. In the Pukhtoon cultural context this was difficult, as it was never done before by anyone. The interveners therefore initiated a dialogue with the male members of the community (usually a Jirga). The interveners educated the Jirga on the importance of the mother and child health and the men finally agreed to allow female health workers to talk to the women on a regular basis and educate them on the subject of family health.

This and other examples depict the use of the institution of Jirga by the NGOs and donor agencies for different kinds of intervention undertaken for the development of communities.

CHAPTER 6

Jirga and its relationship to Laws and Structures

In between voting yes or no for Jirga, one can find similarities and differences between this age-old tribal system and the contemporary systems

JIRGA AND MODERN JUSTICE SYSTEMS

The modern justice system in this region is based on a few distinguishable elements that combine to form the whole system. These can be identified as:

- A **Prosecution System**—Police, Magistrates, and similar bodies
- A **Legal Framework**—Sets of laws enforced in the country
- An **Adjudicating Body**—Various tiers of the judiciary
- An **Implementation Body**—Law enforcement agencies

The legal framework is further divided into the following:

- **The Criminal Procedure**—adopted to process the cases involving crimes specified in the code, such as robbery, murder, assault, etc.
- **The Civil Procedure**—adopted to process the cases involving civil disputes between citizens and institutions.
- **The Penal Code**—defines the extent and nature of punishments for violation of each law.
- **Evidence Laws**—the process and method of recording and evaluating evidence in a certain case before a verdict is reached.
- **Local and Special Laws**—adopted periodically, i.e. the Traffic Laws, Industry, and Labor Laws, etc.

In comparative ways, the Jirga exercises both executive and judicial roles and settles all disputes pertaining to the distribution of land, property, blood feuds, blood money, and other important inter-tribal affairs based on tribal conventions, traditions, and principles of justice. It performs judicial functions while settling a dispute and discharges police functions when a threat to peace and tranquility exists or when there is danger to the life and property of any person in the community.

Pukhtoon Jirga usually deals with local matters and follows a mechanism for dispensing speedy and inexpensive justice. After careful consideration, the Jirga decides the disputes based on available evidence and, for the community, the process and decision hold similar weight and respect as court decisions do in a western legal framework. If needed, the community raises a force called a Badraga[43] to implement the decision.

On the penal side, local traditions known as Rewaj set the standards of punishments for different types of crimes. The punishment can vary from monetary fines to expulsion of individuals from the area, legitimizing murders of revenge, exchange of girls for marriages, or house burning.

Penal laws may vary from place to place and only a few areas have written laws. One example of this is in Kurram agency, which has a charter of laws written in 1944. The laws and precedents of adjoining tribes may influence a particular region, but the suitability of such laws is thoroughly discussed before being adopted.

The tribal laws and tribal systems are complex but workable. They are complex because they are not as uniform as the settled and written laws are, but they work because they are indigenous to the communities and societies who have been practicing them for centuries. Within the complexity, however, it is possible to find ways in which the tribal justice system can be effectively compared to the components of the modern judicial systems.

One distinctive difference between the tribal legal system and the governmental or Anglo-Saxon Legal system is the emphasis on the victim. In the Jirga system, the victim is the focus of any proceeding taken against the offender, whereas in the formal legal system, the state adopts the role of the victim in the proceedings against the offender. Actual victim of the offence is not duly represented in the proceeding and the needs of the victim, including physical rehabilitation, are ignored by the formal judicial systems. Jirga keeps the focus of all proceedings on the victim and his or her needs.

Another distinctive difference is how the systems view punishment. For the criminal justice system, punishment is a primary outcome. Tribal Jirga, on the other hand, continues to maintain its focus on the needs of the victim: the aspect of punishment is considered secondary.

---

43 Malak Nazakai Bajaur Agency

LAWS AND THEIR NATURE

Local laws, like in most traditional systems, change every few miles, but it is claimed that Pukhtoonwali remains the same throughout the Pukhtoon areas. Since there is no codified form of the laws and rules of Jirga or Pukhtoonwali, it is difficult to comprehensively articulate the laws at this stage. Most writers who have written about the code of Pukhtoonwali have written with reference to the penal laws only, while the processes have been noted as indigenous patterns of dispute resolution and adjudication of justice.

In fact, in the face of a desire to institute uniform laws through a system of central governance, the laws prevalent in tribal and traditional societies of the Pukhtoon belt have been undermined in the recent past, identifying the laws of Pukhtoonwali as only the personal and family laws. The code of Pukhtoonwali, however, remained an all-encompassing framework to regulate life in a loose confederation of independent tribal Pukhtoons before the idea of turning the Pukhtoon belt into a nation-state transpired. For this reason, the areas of the Pukhtoon belt under the influence of the British got special statuses as "Federally Administered Tribal Areas" or "Provincially Administered Tribal Areas," which allowed Jirga to play a dominant role in the social regulation and adjudication of justice. Other areas, like Peshawar and its surrounding districts, were merged with mainstream Pakistan at the outset. Since Afghanistan didn't see a fully functional system of government until late, Jirga and the code of Pukhtoonwali remained quite functional there.

In the following sections, we will compare the code of Pukhtoonwali with reference to the legal code prevalent in Pakistan to see how different processes identified under Pukhtoonwali adjust to the fields of a modern legal framework.

Civil Code and Criminal Code

In Pakistan, the Civil Procedure Code (CPC) deals with civil matters only, while the Criminal Procedure Code (CrPC) deals with crimes. As is clear from the names, they both are procedural laws while the Pakistan Penal Code or PPC is a substantial law imposing punishments on violations of laws. In the Pukhtoonwali, which is generally referred to as the "Pukhtoon Code of Ethics", elements of legal distinctions can be identified as follows.

As "Dushmani" or enmity is a distinctively established institution of the Pukhtoonwali, all interpersonal disputes, other than professional theft or robbery, are considered civil in nature.

In the Pukhtoon code, there is little distinction between the civil matters and the criminal matters because it presumes that all civil disputes would lead to criminal offenses. Since the meaning and interpretation of justice is vastly left to the individuals in a Pukhtoon society, it is up to the victim and not the state or society to define the harm done to him, and in turn demand undoing of the harm by the offender. The term "Badal" therefore refers to return, exchange or a reply and not vengeance or strictly revenge. Therefore, a civil offence, if not dealt with justly or diligently will inevitably lead to violence by one or the other party.

Theft and robbery that appear to be done by professionals are considered as crimes against society. It is presumed here that the offender would not have a previous relationship with the victim and the offence would be done in exclusion. Penalties for such crimes are severe in Pukhtoonwali as no mercy is granted the offender.

The judicial system of the state is based on a "crime and punishment syndrome." In this case police apprehends the accused under the law, evidence is produced before a judge, and punishment is announced to the offender. The state becomes the victim in this case and the law forgets the actual victim. The legal system should actually be based on the correction of problems, but that is not happening. The needs of the victim and those of the offender in the aftermath of an offence are lost during the process of adjudication of justice.

In the tribal system, although there is a concept of exemplary punishments for the offenders, there is also an overwhelming concept of meeting the needs of the victim as well as the offender. The practices of restorative justice, though little visible, are very much a part of the tribal judicial system under a purer form of Jirga..

Laws of Evidence and Truth-Telling

Laws of evidence in the Jirga system vary from place to place. Evidence of a person is taken on the face of the statement so given before the Jirga.

Each party has the right to produce evidence, and state before the Jirga what is considered right by that party. The Jirga examines such evidence and puts cross-question. to the witnesses, more like in a case of an inquiry rather than a judicial proceeding. Witnesses are rarely brought up against the other party. False evidence puts the witness in a direct controversy not only with the Jirga but also with the opposing party.

At times specific types of evidence are declared inadmissible for a particular case. For example, in some areas, evidence from a nighttime murder is not taken into consideration for the accusation of a person. This is probably because these places did not have electric lights in the past, thus making the identification of the accused doubtful. As people settled scores in the nighttime while shifting the blame onto someone else, the communities decided that all individuals and families would be responsible for their personal security during the night.

Taking an oath, or "Qasam," in the name of God or on Quraan[44] is a common form of evidence usually taken as a proof of the statement of one party or the other. When the dispute is about a certain issue in which little proof can be found, such as when the person holding evidence has died, an oath by the claimant party is enough assurance to the community of the firm belief by the claimant in their rights. In some cases when such claims of one party are contested zealously by the defending party, the same oath can be served to the defending party. Generally, there is hardly any scope for a contrasting oath by both the parties.

The demand of an oath or the offer of a counter oath is the final proof after which the matter can go only for a full-scale enmity. Even after taking the oath, the parties may not be ready to refer the matter for arbitration because of a fear of losing the case. In case an oath is demanded by one party and taken by the other, the matter must then be settled immediately.

An aspect of the cultural paradigm of Pukhtoonwali is the sanctity of the spoken word. Most businesses are run on verbal assurances as opposed to written records. Trust in spoken agreements is considered a great virtue of Pukhtoons. Coupled with a reference of religion, it should serve as an ultimate assurance.

Interestingly, a more credible oath than the oath involving God is the oath a man takes on his wife. Again, the cultural paradigm binds husbands with their respective wives in an extraordinary personal relationship, such that a man would be pained to say, if I am false, my

---

44 The Holy Book of Islam

wife may become illegal to me. This kind of oath is rarely taken but is absolutely trusted among the contesting parties.

Throwing an oath is another phenomena practiced during dispute resolution. When finding no other clues, one of the parties or the Jirga may throw three stones on the ground and declare that anyone telling lies would have his marriage dissolved. Such a practice can play wonders. Here each stone is considered as a one time announcement of divorce by the person who is expected to say the truth to keep his marriage secured from a social divorce. It may be noted that in Islam, a thrice-made public announcement of divorce by a man dissolves the marriage permanently.

Penal Laws

There is a lot of criticism regarding the penal laws of the tribal system as well as the Islamic laws. The system of punishments in the tribal laws is not as comprehensive and uniform as one would expect. The punishments prescribed by the Jirga fall in two categories: death, exile and house burning, or reparations.

A death sentence, which is quite common in the purely tribal places, is not permissible where there is an external governmental control over the tribal laws. Even in the tribal areas associated with an external government, however, killing or murder is taken as a right of a party seeking "Badal", a form of revenge based on justice. In the purely tribal areas, a death penalty can be announced for a variety of crimes including robbery, kidnapping for ransom, deliberate murder of an innocent person, and adultery. Other than a death sentence, a Jirga can announce the forced exile of a person and burn the house of a proclaimed offender.

The second category of punishments is that of compensatory nature where the party at fault is expected to undo the harm done to the victim, or monetary fines are imposed on the parties. Among the compensatory punishments is the much-criticized tradition of "Sawara," extending a girl in marriage to the victim family.

Interestingly, in the purely tribal setup, there is no scope for announcing jail to an offender, as there are no jails in the tribal communities. In the tribal areas associated with the government, the concept of jail is present, and there the Jirga does not have any powers to announce a death penalty to any kind of offender.

Decisions and Treaties

It may be noted again that in the basic legal system of Pukhtoons, there is hardly any correct translation for the word "decision" as most of the outcomes of external interventions in a dispute must reach an agreement between the parties. Thereafter such decisions are self-sustainable and the onus of their implementation lies mostly upon the parties.

Parties carrying enmity in the Pukhtoon areas can only conclude their enmity through "Rogha". Lexically Rogha means a healthy agreement. The word "decision" is not found in the popular Pushto rhetoric. The term used for a decision is called "Faisala" which is original to Arabic language[45].

An interim decision by the parties regarding their issue can become a truce or a treaty, usually a verbal agreement well known to the whole community and equally respected by all.

Remedial and Compensatory Jurisdiction of Jirga

One of the distinguishing features of Jirga as a court or jury is its extraordinary jurisdiction. This power to address the basic questions arising out of a conflict situation is not enjoyed by any other legal institution so clearly. The modern legal code is based on the legal framework where the judges cannot go out of the bounds of law, while Jirga has no such limitations. The focus of Jirga, therefore, is to address the harms done as a result of an offence or conflict by both the parties. Jirga then proposes to undo such harms as much as possible. This undoing of harms could be symbolic as well as substantial, but the natural endeavor of the Jirga process is to look at the harms done during a conflict situation so that the offending parties can take remedial measures.

In symbolic ways, Jirga imposes upon the offender party a public apology, a Nanawatay or a voluntary offering by the offender to the victim party for doing "justice under sympathy". The offender party doing a Nanawatay thus offers itself in the humble sense of justice to the victim party, restoring the powers of victim party to take revenge and expressing an apology for the wrongs done. Mostly this is a symbolic gesture, but it actually is acted out such that the victim party

---

[45] Mr. Noorul Amin, known Pushto scholar from Swabi area

at each step is assured the restoration of honor and dignity as equal human beings.

Secondly, besides the symbolic compensation, Jirga also enjoys the jurisdiction of requiring material compensation to the victim party. Jirga can allow a financial penalty to be imposed upon the offender party, the money going to the victim party. It can also take care of the rehabilitation process of the victim, like sanctioning social security money to the heirs of someone killed. The offender party thus takes the responsibility to raise the children of such victim, sponsor their food and livelihood needs, including schooling. Taking the widow in marriage would be considered a more sustainable rehabilitation.

LOCAL LAWS, STRUCTURES, AND INFLUENCES

The Pukhtoon code of life, Pukhtoonwali, is considered to have almost uniform meaning throughout the Pukhtoon belt of Afghanistan and Pakistan, but local laws vary from place to place according to the differences in geography, climate, and patterns or structures of living. Therefore, the decisions of Jirga also change depending on the local customs and tradition. Each tribe has its own Rewaj, even though the basic characteristics of Pukhtoonwali remain the same across the Pukhtoon belt. The following sections discuss some of the local factors that influence the variations in local laws and the minute aspects of Pukhtoonwali.

Religion and Laws

Pukhtoons are known to be hard core Muslims of their own kind. They are known to strictly adhere to the five times prayers and the annual thirty days fasting, more than any other Islamic group. Their unconditional allegiance to religious practices, frequent references to Islam and religion give them a distinctive place in the religious circles. However, Pukhtoons are equally loyal to their traditions, which form the basis of their legal code. Therefore, it is perceived that whatever is practiced in the Pukhtoon societies would be strictly in accordance with the teachings of Islam. On the ground, however, that is not true. Many Pukhtoon traditions, particularly those related to the family laws, are in stark contrast to the Islamic teachings. Laws of Inheritance, for example, are the most controversial aspect of the code of Pukhtoonwali, because on the one hand Pukhtoonwali conforms to the concept of supremacy of religious laws, and on the other, for various reasons, it blatantly defies the Islamic injunction regarding inheritance rights to women. Efforts of correction of these perceptions lead to the arguments that stagger between religion, culture, and the relationship of the two.

Additionally, there is no evidence that in the recent history conscious efforts were made to address this question of contradictions between the traditional and Islamic laws.

Precedents

Precedent becomes law or a part of Rewaj in many cases. One good judgment of a Jirga or a practice of a tribe can be easily adopted by others, if it is deemed appropriate for another situation. Similarly, under a difficult legal scenario, a precedent of an adjoining tribe may be adopted if it is found suitable.

Structures and Influences

One factor affecting the code of Pukhtoon life in some areas is the presence of feudal structures. The concept of Khan is thought among the tribal societies to be non-existent; however, it is in fact a reality in the society. A Khan means an aristocrat of the area, usually one representing its entire people. The Khan is not always a ruthless ruler of the medieval times, but is mostly a benevolent lord, depending and promoting the code of Pukhtoonwali in order to protect his estate and status.

Clergy play an important role in expression of Pukhtoonwali in a local area. One well known religious leader of the area might be successful in promoting a specific school of thought. Many rules of Pukhtoonwali can be modified due to the specific teachings of religious leadership of that area.

Malaks are known to be the historical guardians of Pukhtoonwali and torchbearers of Pukhtoon traditions. These Malaks are usually the Jirga members as well. Due to the influence of foreign governments, like the British, the Russians, and also Pakistanis, the institution of Malaks is patronized by these foreign governments. On one hand they protect and promote Pukhtoonwali, on the other they assure the external governments of their fullest cooperation. Masters of diplomacy, they are regularly paid even by the present government of Pakistan and Afghanistan, a legacy of the British times. Again, like other structures, the factor of Malak is stronger and more dominant in some places than the others.

External Influences on Jirga

External laws or national statutes have affected the institution of Jirga from time to time. One such national statute is the Frontier Crimes Regulation 1901 (FCR).   Federally Administered Tribal Areas presently falling under the administration of the Government of Pakistan were created by demarcating the boundaries between Afghanistan and India, popularly known as Durand Line[46] and are governed through the Frontier Crimes Regulations 1901. The law was introduced as part of the scheme of self-governance extended to these people who insisted that any legal framework must be consistent with the local tribal laws. FCR therefore was designed as a procedural law, empowering the representative magistrate to nominate a team of elders to resolve a dispute by whatever possible means. The magistrate in turn has the powers to alter, modify, or quash a decision if proper procedures are not followed. However, all disputes are referred to the local Jirgas, being the cornerstone of the tribal system.

The FCR 1901 was promulgated to regularize and control the working of Jirga. Its practice for the last one hundred years may be a matter of debate, because some would say that the FCR gave protection to Jirga and institutionalized this exploitative system, while others would say that it is the Jirga, which has enabled the Pukhtoon societies to regulate and move their social lives.   However, it is clear that these external statutes like the FCR did have an effect on the nature and outcome of Jirga, for good or for worse.

The concept of Jirga, however, is independent of these national or external statutes but flexible enough to settle with the external environment.

Jirga and Contemporary Local Institutions

Before the inception of the modern governmental system, communities had indigenous institutions to regulate their community lives. These

---

[46] Boundary established in the Hindukush in 1893 by Sir Mortimer Durand, running through the tribal lands between Afghanistan and then the British India, marking their respective spheres of influence; in modern times, it has marked the international border between Afghanistan and Pakistan.

institutions evolved on a social contract, which fulfilled the needs of that particular society at different points in time. In many parts of India, the practice of Panchayat[47] and the system of Salisi[48] are still in practice. In Pakistan, laws were enacted to regulate the working of Panchayat at the local government level. The practice of the "circle process"[49], "Gacaca[50]", and "family group conferencing[51]" are a few examples of traditional mechanisms used to resolve disputes that are still alive today. Similarly, in the Arab world, the practice of "Sulha" is quite similar to the Jirga of Pukhtoons.

These indigenous practices share a few common threads. One is that most of these practices are old in nature and have been in practice since time immemorial. Second, they suit the local environment and, third, they are applicable only in the local context. Above all these reasons, these traditional practices represent a unique principle of justice, now popularly known as restorative justice. Restorative justice presents a framework in which the needs of the victim, the needs of the offender, and the needs of the society all are taken care of in the aftermath of violence. Restorative justice insists upon repairing the harm done to the victim, rather than focusing on awarding punishment to the offender. This non-retributive and unique characteristic is a factor missing from the modern systems of justice.

Today, the fact that these indigenous practices are kept alive can be attributed to two main factors: the absence of alternative institutions for justice, and the efficacy of the local practice.

Absence of Alternate Institutions

The nation-state system is based on the premise that the state is responsible for the life, security, and development of the society. The modern legal system was built to take care of the issues of peace and security, but more and more countries are realizing the fact that these judicial systems only partially take care of the needs that arise out of a conflict situation. The biggest gap in the modern systems is the absence of a mechanism to look after the needs of the victim in the aftermath of violence. Similarly, governments of underdeveloped countries may not

---

47 Means a jury of five
48 Third party
49 Practiced in North America
50 Practiced in Africa
51 Practiced in New Zealand

have the resources to take care of the issues of good governance in the rural areas. Local and traditional practices often fill in the gaps that the government cannot fill.

Efficacy of Local Institutions

These local institutions have been working for the benefit of the people for many centuries. They have, at times, functioned under a quasi-legal framework because they best suited the aspirations of the people. The notification of FCR 1901 by the British, the Panchayat Laws, and tribal laws in other countries are examples of the fact that various governments realized the importance and good use of the traditional systems. In addition, these governments observed the positive influence that grass-roots participation has on development. Local practices are highly participatory at that level and, thus, contribute to the overall development of a society. Jirga, as a traditional, local practice, has influenced the more modern institutions in the region and is thought by some to be one of the most comprehensive, well practiced, and useful institutions among the non-governmental traditional institutions.

NON-GOVERNMENTAL ORGANIZATIONS AND JIRGA

One aspect of Jirga is that of an opinion making body for community level issues. The Jirga can call for a village level meeting and introduce an issue related to a new situation. The Jirga then organizes the community to address that situation, distributes the work responsibilities among the people, and oversees the implementation of the collective work of the community. An example of such a situation is a Jirga giving the call to people to reinforce the riverbanks for the flood season. This kind of decision-making that happens through the Jirga gives it an important role in community organization.

Can Jirga, in its role as a social organizer, be compared to a modern day concept of a non-governmental organization (NGO)? Some believe that it can. Because Jirga works to organize the community voluntarily, it can be thought of as non-governmental body supplementing the efforts of the government in streamlining civil society. There are, however, some differences between the two.

The concept of Jirga is based on offering voluntary leadership to the community. It is a group of organized people, firmly rooted in their understanding of peace and justice issues in the society, and fully dedicated to the welfare of their people. Because of this commitment and dedication, Jirga often becomes involved in politics as well. On the contrary, community based organizations (CBOs) and NGOs find their strengths in their non-political nature. Unlike Jirga, NGOs and CBOs are formed for specific purposes like health, education, etc.

An NGO or CBO will find financial support from a variety of resources, ranging from local donations, government funds, and the international funds, but in the case of Jirga, the funding has to come from a local pool in the form of a local tax, until the government of some external body offers funding for a special purpose.

Jirga works more like a local government. CBOs and NGOs are subject specific, while Jirga is a quasi-judicial, quasi–executive, and quasi-legislative body striving for the betterment of the society. In comparison to a CBO or an NGO, Jirga at the community level can be seen as a local government that can duly accommodate and support the efforts of NGOs and CBOs. With support of a local Jirga, an NGO can find better reception, more acceptability and zealous participation from the locals as compared to a situation where Jirga might be ignored. Support of Jirga can be obtained by first engaging the Jirga members in activities related to information sharing and capacity building, followed by the process design of the project. Hard and tedious as it might be, there seems to be no better mechanism of a productive social sector intervention than engaging Jirga and its capacity building for sustainable development.

CHAPTER 7

The Way Ahead

During the colonial period, in an "us versus them" scenario, people recognized governance as the system of other side, designed and implemented for the benefit of the colonizers only. Newly independent countries of the present day third world inherited these systems of governance, which were alien to their people. Despite the fact that the new governments were mostly democratic in nature and people were duly represented in governments, there remained a gap between the traditional understanding of society and the one presented by the modern systems. People were faced with the following choices in the postcolonial era:

1. *Forget about the past practices and embrace the new system despite the fact that it was designed by alien people. It is now the most viable way of developing into a responsible nation-state.* This was a difficult choice because of deep-seated resentment and hatred for the colonizers. In addition, the loss of past practices and traditions rubs up against issues of identity, language, religion, and culture—aspects of a society that cannot be replaced or buried without pain and, often, resistance.

2. *Forget about the new system given by the colonizers, and let us get back to our old traditional system.* This choice again was a difficult one. During the colonial times societies often preserved their traditional practices. These traditions, however, were not given much natural space to grow and change and, because of this, began to look remote and backwards. The new times also brought science and technology, a development that became difficult for the old systems to adopt and integrate.

3. *Merge the good traditional practices with the modern times and develop systems best suited for our needs as a responsible nation-state.* Some societies could do this easier than the others because of the cultural resonance they had with their colonial masters. However, in other cases, the gap between the masters and the people was so big that it was difficult to merge the two systems. In addition, the people had little capacity to adopt the modern system or improve the

traditional systems to match the modern times. Thus, the deficiency of human capacity prevented the merger of the two systems.

In some parts of the Indian sub-continent, people were able to adapt to the modern system with little difficulty or reluctance. In the case of Pukhtoons, who mostly lived a more remote and independent life in Afghanistan and the adjoining tribal areas, this factor of dissonance was fiercely present. As a result, in the post World War II[52] era, the gap between the modern and traditional systems did not close as it should have.

Pukhtoons retained and practiced their centuries old traditional systems, Jirga being the most vital one. The status of Jirga was further consolidated by the fact that the British had formally recognized this mechanism as early as in 1901 when the FCR was introduced in the Tribal Areas, buffering the boundaries between British India and present day Afghanistan. This recognition by the British, even today, is seen as a sign of victory for an indigenous system of society. The legitimacy gave the Pushto-speaking people the confidence to continue their practice of Jirga and to insist upon maintaining their indigenous system, rather than converting to a new British or Russian model of governance.

Of course, the system of Jirga both at the community as well as the governmental level did not improve as much as it needed to in order to compete with the requirements of the modern governmental systems. Rather than allowing itself to decay, Jirga kept itself as a useful tool for sustaining a bare minimum standard of social contract. The formation of Loya Jirga at Bonn in 2002 proves the point that indigenous local systems can be more sustainable than the fragile modern systems of the present day, particularly for developing countries.

As pointed out above, traditionally Pukhtoon society has been averse to change. Based on the past practices and precedents, Pukhtoon culture or Pukhtoonwali is dominated by references to the past. Other than the traditional folklores of valor or love, there is hardly any scope for a future looking narratives in the Pukhtoon vernacular. References to Masharan[53] and their times, becomes the dominant argument to justify any particular situation.

---

[52] WW II is considered as a reference time of de colonization
[53] Elders, and forefathers

However, it is a fact that things change! Change can be seen in Pukhtoon society, particularly in the urban areas. There is a remarkable difference between the urban elites and the rural poor of the region. The forward-looking people of Kabul share only the language with the rural people of Kunar, for example. Even the language of the urbanites is more sophisticated than the rural ones. Similarly, the culture of Pukhtoons residing in the settled areas of North-West Frontier Provinces, particularly, Peshawar, Mardan, Swabi and Kohat is quite different from the people of adjoining tribal areas of NWFP.

One area of change is around the exclusion of women. The veil for women can be seen as a yardstick to gauge if there has been any departure from the old approach of gender exclusion. Peshawar and Kabul are two major cases where Pushto speaking people have not only reconciled with the idea of schooling for girls, but they are the flag bearers in advocacy for female emancipation. One can even hear reference to the Honor Killing issue. Some critics might argue that the pace of this change is too slow. The fact remains, however, that in the capitals of these Pukhtoon societies, there is enough space now to highlight this human plight and argue for social change in a non-violent manner.

In contrast, in the rural areas, it is still difficult to negotiate with people to change their ways of living. In the recent past, after the overthrow of the Taliban in Afghanistan, this question was repeatedly asked, why are the women in Afghanistan still wearing veils? We found many women jealously guarding their right to veil, and others who hated the ones without a veil. To them, the veil is a means of security and respect, an aspect of status quo that is always so difficult to break.

Improvement in education and economic growth are said to contribute positively to social change. Unfortunately, both these things are missing from the Pukhtoon social structures, particularly, the rural ones. With one of the world's largest refugee populations[54], Afghanistan has been in civil war for the last three decades. Most of the present generation of Afghans is not literate and the economy remains practically non-existent. The situation in NWFP is somewhat different, as the region has seen comparative stability in the recent past. Change and progress therefore are easier for the Pukhtoons of NWFP and the

---

[54] During early eighties, (millio Afghans were registered as refugees in Pakistan. Situation of Iran and Central Asian states was similar.

tribal areas than for the vast majority of rural Pukhtoons in Afghanistan.

Another factor hindering the process of social change is the state of feudalism in developing societies. Feudal structures keep the social order as remote and backward as possible, for the benefit of those in power. Fortunately, in the Pukhtoon societies, the element of feudalism is much less present than in neighboring areas, specifically in Punjab and Sindh provinces of Pakistan. One reason for this could be that, due to mountainous areas, the land holdings are not as large as the ones in the plains areas. Another possible reason is that the high esteemed, independent, and arrogant nature of Pukhtoon individuals has resisted expansion of feudal attitudes in the Pukhtoon societies.

What then is Jirga's role in the process of social change? Jirga, the dominant social institution that guides the lives of Pukhtoons, comprehensively defines all dimensions of life such that individuals can live only within the framework defined by the traditional Pukhtoon culture, i.e. Pukhtoonwali through the Jirga. Even a religion like Islam is subjected to confirmation by the culture and traditions. The famous saying of Wali Khan[55] describes the deeply rooted culture of that region: "we are Muslims since last 1400 years and Pukhtoons since thousands of years and human beings even before that". Relying on this Pukhtoon narrative of history, it implies that we are human beings first, Pukhtoons second, and lastly Muslims. For Pukhtoons, attachment to the past is the norm, as opposed to looking to the future. Jirga then will challenge any move towards social change unless necessitated by circumstances.

Fortunately, the process of Jirga relies wholly on the establishment of communications, a medium that binds the Pukhtoons to continue talking, even to their worst foes. It is the mastery of this art that Jirga upholds, offering a culture of peace and tolerance. Negotiation is the Jirgamars hobby and pleasure and they will always appreciate good negotiators. Jirga, therefore, can be engaged for any kind of topic attractive to the outside world. Beyond negotiation, Jirga would recognize only a war as a natural compulsion forced upon them, obliging them to fight it out. Forcible occupation to them would remain a temporary phenomenon, an opportunity to get back to their traditional system.

---

55 Pukhtoon nationalist leader

As a traditional institution, Jirga has been tested over the centuries in the culture's exposure to alternative systems and pressures to change. What is the path for Jirga amidst these unavoidable dynamics? In this chapter we will discuss some of the critical issues facing the practice of Jirga and suggest a path of reinvigoration and change.

CRITICAL ISSUES

Those who are disenchanted with Jirga often regard it as an old tribal institution that has outlived its utility in modern times. Critics cite Jirga members' turning against the innocent and vulnerable particularly where the Jirga system, applied in combination with the governmental legal system, becomes a tool for manipulation. Or, Jirga is wholly discredited with stories of Jirga members receiving bribes. However, concrete arguments against Jirga and the Jirga system do emerge from the broadly negative stories. These arguments can be broken down into four general themes: unwritten nature, an outdated institution in the modern nation-state system, violation of fundamental human rights, and abuses of contemporary institutions. The following sections will explore the basis of these arguments.

Jirga's Unwritten Nature

Jirga receives criticism for its informal nature, an informality that provides formal structure for those living under it. The laws and procedural rules of a Jirga are un-codified, unstructured, and loose enough to be easily understood and uniformly practiced by the people. Written records of Jirga do not generally exist. One can find some of the written records of Jirga processes and the local criminal, civil, and penal laws in the tribal belt, but even this documentation is not as credible as one would want it to be. For example, the local laws of Kurram Agency in the NWFP were compiled by an English Political Agent[56]. These laws are still referred to by various Jirgas undertaking dispute resolution. The documents are available to a few of the upholders of Pukhtoonwali and are referred to occasionally, but they have never been recognized as a credible basis for local laws.

---

[56] "Turizuna" compiled in 1944 by the then Political Agent Lieutenant Colonel W. C. Leper.

In general, there is an absence of written references and records for Jirgas to uniformly determine how to deal with issues. This is in contrast to the court system that is based on legal evidence and executed according to written legal procedures and decisions. Clearly, pros and cons exist for both systems. The unwritten nature of Jirga law provides enough for the jury to keep in sight the end product, which is an expansive view of social justice. Its looseness also provides flexibility in the socio-legal framework and gives opportunities for growth and improvement. The court systems, on the other hand, while having clarity in design and procedure may become hampered by its own rigidity and lose sight of its original purpose of justice.

As much as a source of richness, the unwritten nature of Jirga laws is one big setback to the Jirga in the eyes of the outside world. How can the Jirga system be formalized? We believe this is possible to some extent and will address the codification of Jirga later in the chapter.

An Outdated Institution in the Modern Nation-State System

The present day nation-state system has done two things to societies around the world. It has demarcated the national boundaries and it has encouraged some form of democratic or semi-democratic system to run societies' internal affairs. So far there is evidence that the nation-state system, earlier in the multi-polar and bipolar world and now in the unipolar world, has successfully reduced and almost eliminated boundary disputes between nations. On the economic and commercial front, innumerable treaties and associations have facilitated a rules-based relationship between people.

Internally, countries have developed legal frameworks to suit the needs of local people. These internal systems have helped societies streamline many complex issues and systems required to establish a social order in a modern, industrialized, and increasingly global, society. We have also seen a sharp increase in conflicts within countries and societies in the last fifty years. This internal conflict situation can be seen as a direct result of systems of governance or the lack thereof. These systems of governance may be seen as somewhat democratic, but in practice, most of these systems are criticized as being autocratic, dictatorial, bureaucratic, imperial, and aristocratic.

To support the local systems, more and more efforts are being made to promote social organization at the grass-roots level. Most of the international donor agencies are supporting the creation of NGOs, CBOs (Community based organizations), WOs (Women Organizations) and VOs (Village Organizations), forming a base for community organizations to empower the people and organize social groups.

Jirga, in such an advanced age, is introduced as an outdated institution. Side by side, some governments in the past have made efforts to streamline local informal institutions and merge them with the regular local order. These efforts, however, did not prove to be very fruitful. Two reasons are noted for this. Firstly there are no clear and uniform definitions of the terms used in relation to Jirga. Even the term Jirga itself can mean different things to different people under different situations. The use of such terms in legal papers means more confusions rather than clarity. Secondly, although the law making process involves final approval of laws by the elected representatives of people, it does not take into account due process of stakeholders' consultations. The laws are drafted through desk reviews by technocrats who find little time to apply reality checks to their proposals. To design a law meant to facilitate social change, rather than force it, a relatively long-term process needs to be initiated, which can take care of many needs of the subject of such a law.

Fundamental Human Rights and Jirga

Jirga is also criticized for laws that violate certain areas of human rights. One criticism comes from the legal community that insists that the accused must be given enough rights to defend him or herself. The Jirga process does not take care of this aspect as seriously as the national legal system. However, this argument is countered by the claim that most legal proceedings do not do enough to punish or create justice because the laws are too lenient with offenders. Members of the legal community also posit that legal practitioners argue cases based on law, whereas in the local tribal set up, there is no scope for a qualified legal council.

The second criticism of the Jirga system comes from advocates of fundamental human rights as enshrined by the United Nations Charter. While similar criticisms could also be levied at the contemporary legal and policing systems where cases of torture and judicial killings are frequent, there is no doubt that traditional Jirga laws violate human rights as defined by the international community. One example is the Jirgas recognition of traditions like Sawara, where a girl is offered from one family to another as a way to reach conciliation. This occurs whether or not the consent of the girl is obtained. Even if the girl consents, there is little room for free choice due to strict adherence to the norms of society. This will be an important practice to examine as Pukhtoons look to preserve the Jirga tradition.

As integral a source of communication as Jirga is seen by some, we will have to learn to negotiate this source of frustration from the outside world, if we want to avoid enforcement of an equally flawed system based on a legal framework as is practiced elsewhere.

Abuses of Contemporary Institutions and Jirga

Local traditional systems like Jirga do exist in almost all societies in one form or the other. Examples of Panchayat in Punjab and India, Salisi system in India, Sulha in Arabs and similar such systems of central Asia, keep coming to our notice. The critics of Jirga sometimes try to compare and ridicule all of these local systems for want of a more logical and understandable legal system. On closer examination, however, one realizes that not all of these systems are uniform in any way. Each local system has its own distinctive characteristics and each has its own base of acceptability within the communities in which it is practiced. For example, the Panchayat system of Punjab can be identified as a typical jury of five people who do not undertake mediation in any sense, but rather conduct their proceedings like a court and announce punishments in a more sovereign manner. Jirga, in contrast, is much more versatile in its role and responsibilities. As a representative institution of the people, Jirga is much more than a jury, and is much more answerable to the community.

Similarly, a local practice in the province of Sindh has recently caught the attention of media in which cases of moral turpitude like adultery are decided by a group of people from within the community[57]. As a result of an accusation by someone, a panel of local elders decides the fate of a girl and a boy involved in an illicit relationship, either to acquit or convict. The only punishment for this kind of an act is a

---

57 The tribal Justice System must be abolished or amended: 19 August 2002, Source; http://web.amnesty.org/ai.nsf/recent/ASA330182002

death penalty implemented by the same panel of people, more popularly known as Karo-kari. This panel is called a Jirga, a misnomer by all standards. It is not clear how and from where the Sindhi language adopted this term of Jirga, which is purely a Pushto language term.

More recently, this kind of a "Jirga" is being opposed by civil society organizations and a federal law is being implemented to discourage this practice. The term is again confused with the practice of honor killing, a norm present in tribal and local settings all over the region.

This raises the question of how Jirga can distinguish itself and also avoid being manipulated by the bad press other traditional, indigenous practices receive. Certainly its unwritten nature contributes to the tendency for misrepresentation and negative publicity. As Jirga becomes more documented and formalized, Pukhtoons will have firmer grounds on which to argue and negotiate for the continuation of Jirga in their communities.

JIRGA, LOYA JIRGA, AND THE NATION STATE SYSTEM

Known for its roots in the Jirga headed by Qais Abdul Rashid during the early days of Islam, or the era of Mir Wais or Ahmed Shah Abdali in the recent times (18th century), Loya Jirga is believed to be a long tradition of Pukhtoon culture.

The Bonn conference of the Afghan Loya Jirga was a gathering to discuss and finalize the framework for an Afghan national government. This conference brought to the limelight the word Loya Jirga for the first time as all the major news networks carried web pages giving information on the history, composition, and role of Loya Jirga as an indigenous Afghan national institution.

A strong argument in favor of the Loya Jirga was aired saying that after three decades of civil war, Afghanistan was still in ownership of an indigenous and workable institution for bringing their national aspirations on a single platform. Some recent studies have also documented that from time to time the Afghan Loya Jirga has worked as a constitution making body[58].

Loya Jirga is a representative body at the highest level of the area, or region. It is not a permanent body as some might think but may be

---

[58] Doctorate thesis by Dr. Misal Zada of Peshawar University, P-205

called from time to time, when larger issues of supreme national interest are to be looked into.

The term Loya Jirga is not restricted to the Afghan national context, as many regional groups of Pukhtoon tribes use the term with their respective prefixes (in Pushto). A grand Jirga of Swabi district for example is called as a "Loya Jirga of Swabi", or when all the tribal agencies in the FATA get together to consider an issue of their collective interest, they call themselves "The Tribal Loya Jirga".

Unlike a Jirga for local level dispute resolution, this kind of a Jirga has a different domain and different objectives. It is always difficult to form a Loya Jirga as one requires a relatively larger logistic base to call such a grand assembly, however, it is best to ask people to send their respective representatives on a date and time fixed to take care of some issue, thereby generating debates at local levels for representation selection matters. Not only is the selection process done from the bottom up, the agenda is also well debated at the local level to give a mandate to the newly formed Jirga to represent the aspirations of these local tribes or clans at the larger platform.

In Afghanistan, under the new constitution, there is a provision for a bicameral legislature consisting of Wolesi Jirga or House of Commons, and the Meshrano Jirga or House of Elders. The Wolesi Jirga comprises of 250 seats directly elected for a term of five years and the Meshrano Jirga is composed of one representative from each provincial council, one representative from each district council, and a number of presidential nominees; including two representatives of Kuchis (nomads) and two representatives of the disabled; half of the presidential nominees are to be women.

Under this constitution, the government may convene a Loya Jirga on issues of independence, national sovereignty, and territorial integrity. It is comprised of the members of the national Assembly and chairpersons of the provincial and district councils who have the power to amend the provisions of the constitution and prosecute the president.

The Pukhtoon cultural system, as explained earlier, has always been based on local as well as personal autonomy. This codification of Afghan Loya Jirga by the government therefore has become a subject of much debate in Afghanistan as the new law has restricted the process of representation from an autonomous, bottom up manner to a top down process. This will definitely affect the efficacy and popular legitimacy of the institution. However, this also gives an opportunity to try to test codification of certain other laws as well. Care must be taken to keep the processes of stakeholder consultations at the heart of any such step. The more we empower the stakeholders, the more sustainable and credible our efforts are likely to be.

JIRGA AS A LIVING INSTITUTION AT DIFFERENT LEVELS

At the community level, if we distinguish between different types of Jirgas, we find that there are three distinct shades of Jirga.

First is the practice of Jirga as a dispute resolution body in urban areas where the governmental systems are well in place, people are well educated, and yet they somehow associate with Jirgas voluntarily or otherwise. In the urban areas, the market disputes in the transport business class, the vendor class, or the real estate class make use of this institution quite normally. Side by side, one can find other options of dispute resolution due to the legal and administrative framework of the government. The legal framework, including the police and lower judiciary, recognizes the efforts of such Jirgas only as an informal institution with little legal value. True as it is, the government agencies do not honor anything like this unless the case is built under the regular law of arbitration or an agreement is turned into a consent degree through a court of law. Therefore, all such activities of the Jirga are finally registered with the government on prescribed stamp papers to get legal protection.

This kind of urban Jirga lacks a uniform, understandable, and logical process from which to operate, and has been largely taken over by the inflexibility and lack of creativity of people leading such Jirgas. To the consumers, as stakeholders, this kind of a Jirga may become coercive with the only available recourse being the mainstream judicial bodies, a process more expensive and painful than the Jirga option. The urban class, already encumbered by a faster pace of life, has little time to deal with unresponsive and rigid associations, so they learn to live with exploitation.

The second practice of Jirga is done in the tribal areas and those places where the influence of the government is relatively low. Jirga in such areas is recognized legally as a dispute resolution body at the community level. Under the FCR 1901, Jirga has the powers to try all kinds of cases, whether civil or criminal and announce punishments.

This Jirga law has been under heavy criticism by the urban class. However, for the last one hundred years, this law has been practice and many shortcomings of the processes involved in the operation of FCR 1901 are already clearly identifiable. A correction of these shortcomings will help improve this law and bring definite improvement in the situation.

In these areas, all development activities should receive consent of the concerned influentials titled as Malaks, before being launched by the government. Usually these Malaks also carry the torch of Jirga to work as a medium between the government and the people. The title of Malak is associated with the Lungi or financial allowance that governments in the past fixed for the elder Malaks whose titles stand inherited by the present generation of Malaks, some of whom are well-respected Jirga people even today. Introduction of adult franchise in the tribal areas and now the planned elections will definitely introduce new stakeholders and empower the people, but the government is hardly expected to fully respond to the needs of common people in the medium term. Even if bypassed by the legislative actions of the government, Jirga will remain an effective tool for people to regulate their day-to-day business for a long time. To introduce a more sustainable social change, the government of Pakistan will need to invest more energy to understand the dynamics of social change, and to make the change valuable both for the government as well as the people of tribal areas. Government will have to allow, rather than the stereo type legislation for the tribal areas, a more innovative strategy to engage the tribal people and their leaders to explore and adopt options which can prove sustainable in the long term.

A third kind of a Jirga is at those places which are still not open to governmental controls either due to inability of the government to offer services such as roads, education, and water supply to the people of these areas or because of the issues of territorial jurisdiction. Areas like Tora Bora in the southern Afghanistan and Teera Valley in the northern Pakistan can be cited as examples. In the absence of the government's regulatory mechanism, people of such areas rely completely on the processes of Jirga as a form of self-government.

Force is an easy tool to use when the problems appear very specific and identifiable, but when the problems are with our own understanding of the complexities of life; it becomes our duty to understand others' worldviews. Any intervention of the government in these areas will definitely require the support and agreement of concerned Jirgas. It is therefore essential that the governments understand the worldview of the people supporting Jirgas. Jirga is not a simple phenomena; it is complex, tricky, and involves detailed processes. Any future plan to introduce governmental controls for the areas practicing Jirga will require detailed studies of the subject and consultation with the stakeholders before launching any plans. If this does not happen, the dissonance we experience between the laws introduced by the British and local customs will be repeated in this case as well.

The Government of Pakistan under its "Devolution of Power Plan 2001" has introduced a body named "Musalihat Anjumans" or "Musalihat Jirga" at the union councils' level with a mandate to undertake dispute resolution through the processes of "Alternate Dispute Resolution" including mediation, arbitration, and conciliation. This initiative is applicable to the regular government controlled area only, but the processes identified in the law have been left for communities to put in practice without any further institutional arrangements for its proper implementation. In most cases, these bodies are not even notified, and where they exist they are doing peacebuilding interventions at their whims. Even the government officials undermine these efforts because of their lack of understanding of the subject. Such initiatives of the government need to be supported by expert bodies so that our experience of regulating community-based processes is turned into a success.

LEGAL SPACE AND JIRGA

Jirga at different levels can be codified. As seen in the above cases, the law for the Afghan grand Jirga has been somewhat codified and the bicameral legislature has also been given the name of Jirga with prefixes. Similarly, the prefixes used for the district level Jirgas and region wide Jirgas are examples of its codification. The dispute resolution Jirga has also been codified in many instances. The FCR 1901[59] is one example. Similarly, in many places local laws are well known and accepted by the communities as substantive laws of the area.

Different Jirga processes can be codified through different stages. In the first stage, we need to agree on uniform definitions of terms

---

[59] Jirga Laws by Ashfaq Ahmed

understood by people from different areas and regions. In case of a difference of definition, there must be different names given to each definition. For example, the Sindh High Court, after observing many cases of honor killing, banned the institution of Jirga. As a result, now in Sindh it is illegal to use the term Jirga. No one knows how a jury system with a predominantly feudal structure came to be called a Jirga. If specific kinds of Jirgas are codified after a well considered and researched argument such definitions can help the external institutions understand and respect the centuries old tradition of Pukhtoons, owned by a large mass of communities.

Fortunately, because of its practice in more advanced times and societies, many weak sides of Jirga stand exposed. Findings of fair and objective researches can allow us to promote the good side of the picture and correct the weaker ones. The various tiers of Jirga and various levels of its operations, the different domains it enjoys, all need to be given authenticity and confirmation by the outside world so as to make the best use of this traditional practice.

Two things must be done to kick-start this process. First the various shapes of Jirga must be named in order to distinguish one from another, as in the case of the names given to the two houses of the Afghan legislature, both suffixed by the term Jirga. Secondly, a dialogue must start with the Pukhtoons regarding the rationalization of Pukhtoonwali, which serves as an unwritten constitution for the Pukhtoon societies. Perhaps as Pukhtoonwali evolved, those maintaining the social institution had no concept of things like education for girls. Now the ideals of many advocacy groups have already started to make inroads into Pukhtoon societies. If changes are brought to the social order, then those changes must merge with the larger social picture. We saw that, in many cases, tribal elders now stand convinced on the issue of education for girls or for allowing outside women access to Pukhtoon women on health care issues, but still such taboos of Pukhtoons remain, creating gaps in the understanding of common Pukhtoons.

REINVIGORATING THE JIRGA

"It depends upon people and integrity of the members of the Jirga, if the Jirga handles the cases with justice and honesty, then it is successful and its future is bright."

Muhammad Rasool

In the fast growing age of globalization, the worldview expressed above, and shared by a majority of our interviewees represents a well-meaning wish and some hope. This statement, however leaves many questions of "how", "what" and "why" of the Jirga system. The worldviews of the outside world expect the code of Pukhtoonwali and the institution of Jirga to articulate, define and debate on many issues, which might look strange to them. What is it then that Pukhtoons need to do to address concerns of the outsiders; and what in turn outsiders need to do to facilitate constructive change of a long neglected traditional society towards development with dignity?

Jirga cannot survive just on good intentions. Jirga will have to recreate its due space if it wants to survive the challenges of the modern world. This will be a process of consolidation of what it already has and a rationalization of the aspects criticized by others providing space for bridging the gap between a traditional and more modern systems. Growth of this will automatically follow.

The proponents of Jirga will be required to bring a better-reasoned case before the outside world in order to be taken seriously. At the same time, keeping aside the question of a viable substitute of Jirga, the opponents of Jirga will need to undertake a cost-benefit analysis before simply discarding a centuries old social practice.

In our discussion, we have tried to see what Jirga is and why it is so. We have also examined how it is practiced now. We saw many roles Jirga plays in simple and still unique ways. We also saw how vulnerable a local system can be when in confrontation with the present day complex issues of social justice. So where do we go from here? Do we want to scrap this centuries old practice, credited for guarding the social fabric, enabling us to survive and allowing us to move on; or do we want to try to modify and improve it to suit present day structures?

In between a 'yes' and a 'no' for Jirga, one can see many options more viable than a surgical insertion of a new legal system. The British overlaid a foreign system on us many decades ago and we are still uncomfortable with that.

Linkages Building

If the Jirga wants to keep itself alive, it will have to come out of seclusion, which has so far been responsible for its protection and growth, but now, this exclusiveness might prove to be a source of decay for the Jirga.

In the fast growing global village, there are many questions and issues that will need to be well addressed before Jirga can find a place in an open and more competitive world. Building linkages with other organizations and agencies will require proper understanding of what Jirga is capable of and how it can collaborate with others.

In the years to come, this unique and effective tribal institution will be operating alongside many new institutions in the shape of NGOs, CBOs and professional organizations. In addition, governments will be gradually extending their controls and government bodies will be formed at the local level. The government will also bring the formation of police and judicial bodies. Jirga will not be able to afford to ignore these challenges or it will bring its own death.

Jirga has seen itself crossing many stages. Once the Jirga was quite independent when it ruled the independent comminutes of Pukhtoon. After sometime different governments of the time started interfering with the Jirga system so as to allow local and cultural practices to find space and adjust into the mainstream legal system. In some cases, the experiment was successful, while in others it failed.

It is clear that all legal systems must take into account the local cultures and practices so that the law suits the temperaments of its people and meets their aspirations. In doing that, we also need to see how Jirga can play a role.

Institutionalizing Jirga

To allow reinvigoration of Jirga, it will need to formally associate with other organizations and bodies in a collaborative manner. To adopt a regular institutional role, to improve its present status, and to be trusted by outside world, Jirga members will have to agree on some basic rules and regulations for the conduct of their business. A formal recognition will take away some of the flexibility and dynamic nature of the Jirga, but at the same time, it will facilitate Jirga to keep playing a constructive role in the development of their societies.

Jirga remained a ruling body in the past and carried its people through the thick and thin of life. In the present times, no organization or body can be as inclusive as Jirga once was. It will therefore have to split itself into compartments and fragments based on the nature of the work it can undertake. The case of the "Wolesi Jirga and Meshrano Jirga" in the Afghan governmental system is a good example of Jirga letting itself break into specialized areas of work. Development of a standard vocabulary with uniform definitions would help Jirga to grow in a more logical manner. The same can be done to the Jirga at the grass-roots level. For example, the peacebuilding Jirga can be given a specialized name and its jurisdiction can be defined to distinguish it from a Jirga involved in development work.

Re-examination of Pukhtoonwali

Pukhtoonwali, the code of the Pukhtoon way of life will have to be re-examined to adjust it to the needs of the present day nation-state system. The ideas and concepts of fundamental human rights of the modern world will have to be given space in the code of Pukhtoonwali. The transition from one system to another is of course a difficult issue, but rather than letting it go to anarchy, Jirga will have to take a lead and negotiate with the outside world so that a voluntary correction is made without much distortion to the core of Pukhtoonwali. Some of the distinguishable elements of Pukhtoonwali will need to be codified to make it a more trustworthy and reliable idea.

Future Role of Women

Pukhtoons are a patriarchal society and, therefore, the role of women is kept invisible. It is interesting to note that in the past, particularly in Pukhtoon rural societies, women did not observe the Purdah in the strict sense as is prevalent in the present times. Women still work in the fields and take the cattle to pasture in the mountains in many areas. Nevertheless, in the urban and semi urban areas, women are subjected to a strict code of seclusion, having their lives limited to the four walls of the house.

The understanding of the insider-outsider dynamics of social sector interventions need to be made more understandable to the Pukhtoon culture so that it is comfortable working on this more challenging social ground.

The importance of women and their role in society truly came to the limelight in the Afghan civil war, when women were the worst victims of a war fought by men. These women took their children from place to place in the Afghan refugee camps and survived the traumas of that time.

Now in the Afghan national legislature there is a provision for a substantial inclusion of women in the assembly. Similarly, under the local government ordinance in Pakistan, one third of the seats stand reserved for women. The code of Pukhtoonwali will have to explain why it wants to keep a specific segment of women from living a fuller life. What can it do towards this end and what steps should it follow to allow enough space to women so that their due rights are assured. This will also include a deeper examination of Islamic laws and their application in the Pukhtoon belt, where Pukhtoons are called to be loyal Muslims just as the rest of the Islamic world is.

In addition to addressing questions regarding the practice of the old time traditions like Sawara, the society will require to allow women for training and education on many areas including "Women and Child Health", Population Control, and Education Sectors etc.

APPLICATIONS OF JIRGA

Jirga has proven to be an excellent platform to negotiate change. It plays a leadership role in society and is seen by those who are a part of the culture to be a socially responsible institution. It has the power to legitimize or delegitimize the direction of the society. Ignoring the Jirga would mean creating a definite rift and dissonance within the society that would be dangerous to the healthy sustainability of change. The strength of Jirga emanates from its ability to negotiate under all circumstances and maintain the link of communication. Tough as it may be, it also has enormous potential to influence society in a substantive way. As a channel of communication, Jirga provides many indigenous tools and processes to allow a smooth social change in a direction considered better than before.

If empowered through capacity building, Jirga can help move people in directions well prescribed for people for whom so far, due to coming from a state of fear, the best course was to remain averse to change.

Change it must, if it wants to look beyond the lingering threats of assimilation by an invading culture and understand what development can mean. To the development world, this will be a challenge as well as an opportunity to help the long neglected segment of people find a reasonable place in the world community.

For engineering a sustainable process of social change we recommend taking help from John Paul Lederach's framework presented below[60].

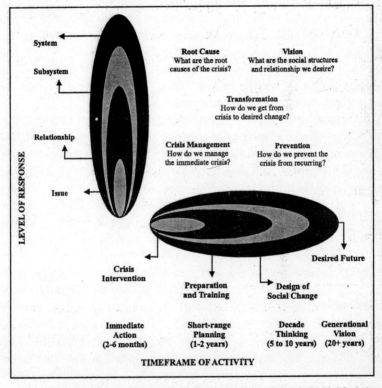

Source: **John Paul Lederach, *Building Peace:* Sustainable Reconciliation in Divided Societies (Washington, DC: United States Institute of Peace Press, 1997), p. 80.**

In this Time of Activity- Level of Response framework, John Paul suggests distinction between immediate issues, relationship building and challenges presented by structures. A proper timeframe is duly required to achieve what cannot be achieved in a short term. The idea

---

60 John Paul Lederach, Building Peace: Sustainable Reconciliation in Divided Societies (Washington DC USIP Press 1997) p.80

is to first categorize the issues in proper contexts and then develop processes and strategies to address needs according to the context in which the subject is under study. In contrast to a reaction based response, this model suggests a proactive approach to a healthy social change; a process which should allow due participation of stake holders, address immediate causes, identify root causes, provide a vision and facilitate transformation in a continuous and sustainable manner. Therefore, beyond troubleshooting, efforts for sustainable social change need to be based on a web of peacebuilding activities to be carried out by a variety of civil society actors as well as the government agencies operating in different time frames.

To allow Pukhtoons full-scale empowerment for participation in the struggle for development and to alter Jirga's collision course, we recommend following John Paul's framework in three ways.

A short-term strategy is prescribed to work with the immediate issues of viewing Jirga as a valuable partner in development. The NGO community and outside interveners can find two kinds of support from Jirga in the immediate term. One is the role of Jirga as a dispute resolution body at the community level. The other is to launch Jirga for the purpose of social change and development. To take a start, the outside world will have to review their notion of considering Jirga as an outdated and useless entity in contrast to their loved concept of Village Organizations (VOs).

Whereas introduction of the concepts of VOs in the Pukhtoon areas are likely to exacerbate the gap between the natives and the outside world in the long run, a strategic collaboration with Jirga will definitely fill this gap in a sustainable way. In fact, a little bit of tailoring of the VO concept can suit well for an already established form of Jirga. The sensitivity to local nomenclature and stakeholder participation is a must for reorganizing the Pukhtoon society for a long-term strategy. Starting a dialogue may be difficult but when a positive relationship is established, it is likely to pay off more than the current models in practice by social sector organizations. The onus of responsibility in the short term lies with the CSOs and NGOs and foreign donors to build a model of intervention through Jirgas. The work of NRDF[61], a local NGO working with Clergy as a forum of

---

[61] National Research and Development Foundation, a Peshawar based NGO and pioneer of "Ulama and Development Concept" www.nrdf.org.pk.

intervention, can be made use of while formulating the model of intervention for Jirga. The acceptance of this idea will require detailed studies by the NGO staff and officials. The NGOs will have to challenge their natural biases and realize that their efforts can prove more effective if their channels of operation (Jirga) have historical roots in the society.

The second phase, a mid term strategy is likely to be tougher than the first, as this will involve doing some extensive and strategic capacity building for the people of Jirga. Again, the onus of responsibility for this activity will lie on the outside world. It is observed that the international bodies, while launching their programs, have pre-designed output and outcome indicators, but the rules do not allow, in most cases, their interventions a life of more than one year. With such a short-term life span, it is difficult to achieve a target of capacity building for such a vast segment of Pukhtoon society. Perhaps a district or area-based strategy to consolidate and test the model and to be subsequently followed by a massive roll out of the program will be a more useful idea.

In the long term, Jirga needs to see if it wants to become associated with the outside world and link itself to the external environment in a constructive way. This will involve the process of institutionalization of Jirga at structural levels. Jirga laws at different levels and for different types of Jirgas will need to be drafted, tested, and implemented such that Jirgas are allowed to evolve and societies are allowed a safe transit from a backward and closed social system to a more forward-looking and scientific one. This long-term strategy is again suggested as an outreach activity by the supposedly more enlightened class of modern civil society organizations. These organizations need to realize that social change, although a positive and much desired outcome of our struggle must follow a pace suitable to the local environment or the outcome of surgical procedures may further confuse the long-traumatized generations of Pukhtoons.

SELECT BIBLIOGRAPHY

- AttaUllah, Qazi, *Da Pukhtano Tareekh (History of Pukhtoons)*, Idara-e-Ishaat Sarhad Peshawar, 1962.

- Bellew, H.W.. *The General Report on the Yusufzais.* Lahore: Sang-E-Meel Publications, 1994.

- Caroe, Olaf Kirpatrick, Sir. *The Pathans, 550 B.C.-A.D. 1957.* Karachi, Pakistan: Union Book Stall,1980.

- Easwaran, Eknath. *The Man to Match His Mountains: Badsha Khan, Nonviolent Soldier of Islam.* Petaluma, Calif.: Nilgiri Press, 1985.

- Grima, Benedicte. *The Performance of Emotion Among Paxtun Women.* Karachi: Oxford University Press, 1993.

- Hart, David M., Guardians *of the Khaibar Pass: The Social Organization and History of the Afridis of Pakistan.* Lahore: Vanguard Books, 1985.

- Misal Zada Professor, *"The Role of Afghan Jirga in Law Making"*, PhD thesis presented to Faculty of Law University of Peshawar

- Obhrai, Diwan Chand. *The Evolution of North-West Frontier Province: Being a Survey and Constitutional Development of N.-W.F. Province, In India.* Peshawar: Saeed Book Bank, 1983.

- Schofield, Victoria. *Every Rock Every Hill: A Plain Tail of the North West Frontier and Afghanistan.* London: Buchan &Enright, 1984.

- Singer, Andre. *Lords Of The Khyber: The Story of the North-West Frontier.* Boston: Faber & Faber, 1984.

- Spain, James W. *The Way of the Pathans._* Karachi: Oxford University Press, 1972.

- Winson, Arthur. *North-West Frontier.* Hutchinson   & Co. (publisher) Limited, 1969.

- Younas S. Fida, *Afghanistan (Jirgas & Loya Jirgas the Afghan Traditions)*, 1997

112

The Way Ahead

Qualitative Research Methodology

- Kvale, Steinar. *InterViews: An Introduction to Qualitative Research Interviewing*. Thousand Oaks, CA: Sage, 1996.
- Robson, Colin. Real World Research: A Resource for Social Scientists and Practitioner-Researchers. Cambridge, MA: Blackwell, 1993.
- Rubin, Herbert and Irene Rubin, *Qualitative Interviewing: The Art of Hearing Data*. Thousand Oaks, CA: Sage, 1995.
- Slim, Hugo and Paul Thompson. *Listening for a Change: Oral Testimony and Development*. Panos, 1993. Philadelphia: New Society Publishers, 1995.
- Smith, Carolyn and William Kornblum (eds). *In the Field: Readings on the Field Experience*. Westport, CN: Praeger, 1996.
- Stringer, Ernest. *Action Research: A Handbook for Practitioners*. Thousand Oaks, CA: Sage, 1996
- Weiss, Robert S. *Learning From Strangers: The Art and Method of Qualitative Interview Studies*. New York: Free Press, 1994.

Web links

Many of the web links identified at footnotes in the main body have expired since we noted them first. However the domain names of the websites carrying the links remain same. Therefore more information on the subject can be accessed from the following links

http://www.geocities.com/khyber007
http://www.meenaswat.com
http://www.peshawar1.com
http://dsal.uchicago.edu/dictionaries/raverty/
http://news.bbc.co.uk/1/hi/world/south_asia/1782079.stm
http://www.afghanland.com
http://www.khyber.org
http://www.jirga.net
http://www.parachinar.com
http://www.nwfp.gov.pk
http://www.khyberwatch.com
http://www.institute-for-afghan-studies.org
www.pakhtun.com